LOST IN AUSTIN

LOST IN AUSTIN

THE EVOLUTION OF
AN AMERICAN CITY

ALEX HANNAFORD

DEYST.
An Imprint of William Morrow

DEYST.

HarperCollins books may be purchased for educational, business, or sales promotional use. For information, please email the Special Markets Department at SPsales@harpercollins.com.

FIRST EDITION

Designed by Alison Bloomer

Library of Congress Cataloging-in-Publication Data has been applied for.

ISBN 978-0-06-325302-5

24 25 26 27 28 LBC 5 4 3 2 1

For Pat and Pete
and Scruff (2007–2023)

CONTENTS

INTRODUCTION

onestly, the Texas capital barely registered as a possible place to stop, even for a night, when my friend Luke and I embarked on a mammoth three-month road trip across America. It was the spring of 1999, when, a week into our journey, we found ourselves in a dingy, sparsely decorated row house in south Philadelphia, hanging out with an aging musician who insisted on seeing the route we'd plotted across the country. "You're not going to Austin?" he asked, gripping our Rand McNally road atlas between yellowing fingers, the butt of his cigarette perched between his thin lips. He could barely conceal his horror at the idea of anyone ignoring Austin on a US road trip. And that's why, on a sweaty afternoon in early May, Luke and I wheelspun an eleven-year-old Pontiac Firebird into the parking lot of a youth hostel on the other side of Town Lake from downtown Austin.

The hostel's manager, Eli, was a bleached-blond ball of energy with thick, dark eyebrows. He showed us an aromatic, twelve-bed, men-only bunk room and the sparse lounge area of the small, single-story building, and then led us through a door to a yard out back where, under the sinking Texas sun, ten twentysomethings were perched on wooden picnic tables, sipping beer and smoking pot. Among them was Danny, a fellow Englishman; two Swedish girls who, like us, were on an adventure across the States; Briton, a slim African American guy with dark sunglasses and beads in his hair who wrote poetry under the nom de plume Phantom of the Hemp Hop; and Derek, a rake-thin twenty-four-year-old white boy with close-cropped mousy hair who played drums in a country band and who was apparently escaping his responsibilities as a father to a young son back home in the Midwest. Derek told us he now dealt drugs to make a living, and Austin, apparently, was the perfect home for his new entrepreneurial start-up—a musicians' mecca where you could rent a bed in a hostel for twelve bucks and rely on a healthy supply of customers for cocaine and weed.

Eli strode over. Four months earlier he'd been living in Denver, but after a relationship with a girlfriend soured, he'd jumped in his old Saab 900 Turbo and hightailed it to Tulsa, Oklahoma, to stay with an aunt, working as a day laborer until he'd saved enough cash to get to Austin. Eli arrived in town with forty-seven dollars in his pocket, went straight to a blues bar, and, that first night, slept in his car. The then manager of the youth hostel agreed to let him clean the floors and toilets in return for a permanent place to stay. He found a job at a nearby Italian restaurant, and eventually took over as manager of the hostel. "Life's good," he told me and Luke that first night. "But I won't be here forever."

Like the rest of us, Eli was restless and already looking around for where to go next. Ultimately, he saw himself opening a restaurant by the ocean in Florida, but for now Austin was the perfect place to pitch up for a while: it didn't have the frenetic pace of other cities, you didn't have to dress a certain way, and despite the heat, people seemed to thrive on being outside, cooling off in its natural water holes and lakes or enjoying live music and the best Mexican food in America.

Derek disappeared inside the hostel and returned with a battered acoustic guitar, then sat on a picnic table and began strumming a folk tune he'd written earlier that day. We all pivoted to watch, blissfully unaware, as the guitar chords echoed out over the lake beyond, competing with the scream of cicadas, of a tragedy unfolding just a few hundred feet away.

A little later, Luke, Eli, and I took a bus downtown and walked along Sixth Street, the thoroughfare of bars, venues, and tattoo parlors that was to Austin what Beale Street is to Memphis or Bourbon Street is to New Orleans. Every open doorway led to a club, live music competing with the voices of doormen enticing customers with "dollar shots." Souvenir stores sold bongs and ball caps and T-shirts that said "Keep Austin Weird," while hours ago police had closed each end of Sixth Street to cars so night owls could take back the road. We bundled into Flamingo Cantina, a dingy reggae and world-beat joint. A back door opened onto a large open-air patio and a stage, where a rap-reggae band with a five-piece horn section was mid-set. We spent hours wandering Austin's streets that night, my T-shirt and jeans clinging to my skin in the sticky heat. We arrived back at the hostel in the early hours of the morning, bleary-eyed, to find three police cars in the parking lot, blue and red lights flashing. Earlier that evening, a fisherman on the lake had discovered the body of a young man, face up at the water's edge—a twenty-one-year-old kid from Utah who, like us, had been staying at the hostel. He'd been missing for a few days and his family had been looking for him; Eli just figured he must have packed up and left without saying anything. We didn't hear much more that night, but the police said that he'd drowned, that he'd taken his own life.

The following afternoon, Eli led ten of us, single file, in silence, across the grass behind the hostel and along a dirt path to the lake and suggested we each pay our respects to our fellow traveler in our own way. Then it began—a ceremony of sorts. A couple of people read poems; someone said a prayer. The rest of us, Luke and me included, stood there, a little bewildered, a silent part of this ritual under the scorching Texas sun; participants in a tribute to a traveler we never knew. I didn't realize then how profound this single event would turn out to be, how the tragic death of a young man in Austin was a singular moment around which my own life would pivot. It had forced a handful of people who barely knew one another to unite against the backdrop of tragedy, and Luke and I knew in that moment we couldn't leave town that day.

It seemed deeply unusual to find yourself in a city that felt more like a small town; a place where strangers would band together to celebrate and mourn the life of someone they hadn't known. I found it almost indescribably moving, to see how this disparate band of travelers had quickly become a community and how Luke and I had become part of that as well. Looking around, I felt that there was something bigger to the situation too. Something about Austin had drawn this man here, and something meant he would end his life here just as I was beginning the next chapter of mine. I wasn't spiritual, but even I thought that this was somehow fatalistic, and in years to come I'd look back and see that it took the death of this stranger to make me fall in love with Austin.

Back at the hostel, Eli was shuffling papers at the front desk.

"We'd like to change our booking," I said. "We want to stay for the week."

Our unplanned extended stay in Austin meant that over the next week I'd get to know the city—and some of our fellow travelers in the Town Lake hostel—a little better. If you were fazed by the searing heat, you just parked up on a quiet, tree-lined road around the back of some apartments and wandered down a dirt path into a wilderness of cottonwoods, oaks, and cedars until you reached a not-so-secret swimming hole to cool off. And there wasn't just one. Austin had swimming holes and spring-fed pools all over town and far beyond in the Texas Hill Country. They had names like Gus Fruh, Sculpture Falls, Campbell's Hole, Deep Eddy, and Krause Springs. From the top of Mount Bonnell, the city's highest point, you could see how Austin lay snug in a bed of vibrant green, how the river, sparkling, carved its way through the middle of downtown, and how the rolling hills kept watch over everything from a distance. Back in London, the winters could be soul crushing, and I'd tired of the thick soup of gray sky that hovered above the city for months on end. Austin, meanwhile, enjoyed three hundred days of sunshine every year. I hadn't seen another city where a greenbelt lay at the very heart of downtown, where people ran laps around a trail that framed a shining lake, and where its residents embraced the outdoors despite the scorching summers. The city boasted the world's largest urban colony of Mexican free-tailed bats—and bat watching, live music, and breakfast tacos had apparently come to define Austin in equal measure.

It felt like we were in America but protected from its worst excesses; a kitsch, retro America-lite where you could forget the real world outside. I'd traveled a fair bit: we lived in Nigeria when I was a kid after my dad's bank job required relocation to Lagos, we'd been all over Europe, and I'd lived in Hong Kong for six months between high school and college. But Austin was unlike any place I'd been before, including other American cities. In 1979, Mom, Dad, and I had flown to the West Coast and driven up Highway 1 to San Francisco, but the closest I'd come to seeing the real "West" of *Young Guns* and *Pale Rider*, which I'd grown up watching as a kid in London, was a tour of the backlots at Universal Studios, where a stuntman, dressed as a cowboy, fell from a two-story saloon after being shot. Now, Luke and I were drinking in bars on Sixth Street in buildings that resembled those very same saloons, but these were actually built in the 1880s, when Austin was a frontier town. We were deep in the heart of Texas, and it felt like that isolation had somehow served to freeze Austin somewhere in the 1950s. Neon signs heralded run-down motels, dance halls, and rock clubs. It was a weird, intoxicating mix of frontier town, hippie holdout, and indie mecca, with too many Mexican restaurants to count.

Eating enchiladas on the covered patio outside El Arroyo, I heard the song "Miles and Miles of Texas"—"I rode up in to Austin the cradle of the West / Just ask any cowboy he'll tell you it's the best." It's a song about a Louisianan who crosses the Red River into Texas, finds love, and makes the state his new home. I was from London, not Louisiana, but I fantasized about living in this old cow town. Sure, at the age of twenty-four, the idea of getting shit-faced in bars every night perhaps had an outsized appeal, but Austin also embodied the notion you could do something different with your life. This was the city of reinvention: exciting, bubbling with opportunity and optimism. It was where a young Janis Joplin got her break in the 1960s playing at a former gas station called Threadgill's, whose owner was the first person in the county to get a beer license, turning the joint into a venue for traveling musicians. It was where another venue, the Armadillo World Headquarters, played host to a performance by Willie Nelson in the early '70s that would help define the "Austin sound" and help cement its reputation as the live music capital; where a teenage Michael Dell started a personal computing company in his garage while studying at the University of Texas and who would go on to become the city's homegrown tech success story. And it was where, while I was busy succumbing to Austin's charms, a cross-dressing homeless man named Leslie Cochran was preparing his bid to become the city's mayor (a race in which he'd come second). Austin was where you could be yourself and make it on your own terms. It seemed like an eccentric city, an outlier, a place so unique I never contemplated it could ever change.

But in the early summer of 1999, I knew very little, really, about this simmering city that had made such an impact on me. I later found that Austin had this effect on a lot of people when they first arrived: you wondered, How could there possibly be another place to rival this? Nineteenth-century storefronts and homes that now served as punk rock bars; twenty-four-hour cafés playing obscure indie records on repeat while hip staff served up migas and Texas toast and bottomless mugs of black coffee; tattooed slackers in cowboy hats and boots; brisket smoked for twelve hours; warm people who rivaled the climate; lakes, rivers, and water holes; opportunity. It seemed like the coolest, most laid-back city I'd ever been to; people came here seeking big, unapologetic, Texas-style living, combined with a cultivated atmosphere that encouraged individual expression. That was the Austin of the tourist pamphlets, anyway: a rose-tinted vision of a place that I guessed was a lot more complex. To really get under the skin of what's become one of America's fastest-growing, most popular cities, you need to stick around awhile.

Within a few days of Luke and me leaving town, a new international airport would open, and in a few years Austin would no longer be America's best-kept secret. Pretty soon, the city would become almost unrecognizable from that place we'd stumbled on more or less by accident in 1999. I wouldn't see Eli again for almost twenty years. A few days after Luke and I headed west in the Firebird toward the New Mexico desert, he quit his restaurant job, packed his bag, and left the youth hostel on Town Lake for the last time, pointing his old Saab in the opposite direction from us, destined for Florida. But, like us, Eli's Austin experience would forever change him. That's what this place does to people.

As I'd stood on the banks of the lake that day listening to the words of a poem I've long since forgotten, it occurred to me that everyone at the youth hostel—including the man whose body had been pulled from the water hours after I'd arrived—was on some kind of journey, possessed by wanderlust, perhaps, or seeking something, lured here to the center of Texas with the promise of excitement, hope, and change. Some saw Austin as a crossroads, a place where they'd decide which direction their life would go next. In the sliding-doors moments that history affords, a planned stop for a night in a city I'd hardly heard of would prove to be life altering.

August 2023

It's summer in New York's Hudson Valley, and more than three years since my family and I packed up our lives in Austin and moved to the East Coast. My wife, Shannon, and I had met at the tail end of an exhausting, alcohol-fueled South by Southwest festival in March 2003, got hitched eighteen months later in a service overlooking Lake Travis, and spent the best part of seventeen years living in Austin. In 2011, our daughter, Olive, was born. At the time it seemed like the perfect place to raise a family. Olive was an Austinite by birth, but so was I by assimilation. I didn't think we'd ever leave.

But by 2019, the city had changed. Property prices, taxes, and rents were soaring; cars and trucks sat bumper to bumper on congested highways; the convection-oven weather had finally taken its toll; and, for us at least, Austin's magic was evaporating in that heat. For nearly two decades, I'd had a front-row seat to the meteoric changes in one of the most rapidly expanding cities in America. The *New York Times* called its real estate market a "madhouse," saying it had forced regular people to act like "speculators." It was the only major growing city in America to have a declining Black population. What's more, it was still trading on its credentials as the "Live Music Capital of the World"—"Austin lets you create a soundtrack all your own," the website for the visitors bureau proclaimed. "So take a look around, and put the Live Music Capital of the World° on your playlist"—yet working musicians couldn't afford to park downtown to unload their gear, let alone live there.

The city's cultural capital was the reason people who relocated there for work were so pumped about it. Was there some bait and switch going on? Yes, its economy was flourishing, but Austin had become a symbol of all things that big cities represent in the best and worst ways—the canary in the coal mine for a huge social experiment where people moved to a place by the thousands, regardless of the impact on traffic, infrastructure, the environment, or the folks who had called it home for generations. Over a relatively short space of time the city had lost the very thing that once defined it: its individuality. Sure, it now had a restaurant scene to rival New York City or London, and there were myriad things to do with your spare time, but a whole host of other American cities boasted the same thing. Austin no longer stood out. It wasn't an outlier. It had gone from being a hippie in flip-flops chowing down on Tex-Mex watching a blues band in some dive bar to a guy in a pressed shirt, Patagonia vest, and Allbirds sneakers eating Japanese-barbecue fusion in an air-conditioned new build.

The French anthropologist Marc Augé distinguished between "places" and "non-places." Places, he said, were closely linked to the culture of the society from which they developed: in Austin's case, African American and Mexican culture and, later, the laid-back hippie culture of the '60s. Non-places, on the other hand, are homogenous spaces that have had that culture eradicated, replaced with a sterile sameness; what we find today in chain stores, hotels, and car parks. Is that what Austin had become? Perhaps. In my view, despite a host of independent coffee shops and restaurants, it wasn't far off.

After three years away it's weird going back to a city I lived in and loved for so long in order to try to report on it somewhat dispassionately. But time and distance afford you a little more perspective. I wanted to find out what had happened to the place I had fallen for so hard and that had shaped my life so profoundly. I wanted to explore how the ghosts of the city's past still haunt it today, how, despite its furious population explosion, Austin plans to secure its future, located as it is on the front lines of climate change. There's so much earth being moved in Austin's construction boom it's a wonder the city hasn't caved in on itself like some giant sinkhole. Austin's physical landscape has changed, almost unrecognizably, and with it, arguably, the city's "soul": those can't-quite-put-your-finger-on-them qualities that made it such a special place to start with. There's a frenetic energy to Austin today that didn't exist before—people rushing to be somewhere, on roads busier than ever, living in a city that could really be anywhere. Gone is the breezy attitude of the old Austinite. But I was also aware that, for newcomers to this city, it could quite possibly be the greatest place they've ever lived.

How do you square those differences in perspective? There is no question that there has been a fundamental change that is irrefutably tragic: at the end of the working day, the see-and-be-seens go to their modern condos scattered throughout this growing city, while the cleaners, street sweepers, bar staff, and line cooks jump in their aging cars and join the lines of traffic out of the city toward home. There's a growing chasm between rich and poor in Austin—those who can afford to live in the coolest city in America and those who work there and want to call it home but can't afford to. And yet people continue moving there in droves, coaxed by the same promises that convinced me to do the same thing so many years ago.

I wanted to go back and attempt to understand what had happened to my beloved city, to look at all the different factors influencing its transformation—gentrification, climate change, guns, the tech boom, its much-hyped music scene—and see what could be learned about the city's past and future. I wondered too about other cities that experienced rapid breaks of tremendous growth—Detroit and San Francisco, among others—and how their cultural identity changed as a result. Was it possible that the magic of Austin had truly been lost, and if so, what next? What created that magic to begin with? And what does America lose when that sense of urban identity is gone? The questions were endless. This book is an attempt to ask—and hopefully answer—some of these questions.

There's a rough timeline I've focused on: the twenty years or so between me "discovering" Austin for myself and my family and me deciding to pack up and leave the city for good. I felt the changes Austin had undergone were just too profound, but I hope my love for the city comes through in these pages. I guess "Austin-ite" will always be a part of my identity.

Since my road trip back in 1999, I've thought a lot about the young lad who died in the lake that night; I've regularly told the story of how Luke and I arrived in Austin planning to stay a night but ended up staying a week because of that tragedy and how that had changed the course of my life. But I didn't know any-thing about him. Who was he? What was his name? Why was he in Austin?

I discovered that Brian Case grew up in Park City, Utah, a ski town. He was the eldest of three brothers—his siblings were twins—and he loved the outdoors: skiing, biking, fishing, and running in the mountains. He was obsessed with music and loved to write poetry. But Brian had schizophrenia, and in 2012, his mother, Jean Baker, self-published a book about it. "What if a per-fect child is born with a time bomb that goes off in his brain at 16?" she wrote. Brian had dropped out of the University of Utah, and by the time he turned twenty, his life was spiraling out of control. He'd been in trouble with the law and had spells of homelessness, but his family held on to a shred of hope when he announced he was going to Austin. Jean had met Brian's dad there in the early 1970s when she moved to the city for college. For her, Austin "sym-bolized love, happiness, and freedom," she wrote. "It holds such irony that Austin was the location of my son's death. Life does in-deed go full circle." The last time Jean spoke to Brian was May 1, 1999; he called her from somewhere in the city and seemed in good spirits. He planned to check into a youth hostel and find work at the University of Texas, her alma mater. Brian's brother Dillon told me Austin could have been a perfect fit for Brian if he had been well. He said his brother had a weird sense of humor and was dizzyingly creative and intelligent, making up hilarious songs on the fly and shooting movies with his video camera. "Brian was full of curiosity, wit, patience, principle, and joy," Dillon said. "As his schizophrenia took over, I think part of his journey to Austin was an attempt to reclaim his dreams from just a few years before. There was hope in his move to Austin. There was desperation too."

On my first reporting trip back to the city, I pulled up in the car park of that youth hostel Luke and I stayed in on the banks of Town Lake, now known as Lady Bird Lake, and found it had closed its doors permanently during the COVID-19 pandemic. It felt like a sign of the times—a prime location on the water's edge was far too salubrious for a backpackers' refuge. But as I sat there lamenting what a city inevitably loses as it grows, wondering what went right, what went wrong, and where Austin is headed next, I recalled a slogan for the University of Texas: "What starts here changes the world." And I thought it should really read: "What starts here changes you."

CHAPTER 1

LESSONS FROM THE PAST

Whenever you move to a new city, of course you're hopeful,
but I think Austin inspired something else—something
more profound—in the people who came here intent on
putting down roots. It did to this Londoner, anyway. There was a
pulse to the city I'd never experienced anywhere else. Plus, there
was this girl.

For two years, since I first stumbled on Austin with Luke in
1999, I'd been plotting my return. The idea of actually living there
permanently seemed, then at least, too unrealistic, but I just knew
I had to get back there in order to explore Austin more. After our
road trip I'd flown back to England and gotten a job working on
the features desk of the *Evening Standard,* London's biggest newspaper, and I figured writing a story about Austin would be the
easiest way to get back to Texas in the near term.

In 1999, several people had told me about the SXSW festival—
"Spring break for the music industry," they called it—an incubator
for new bands where talent scouts from record labels around the
world descended on Austin to see new acts at various bars and
venues across the city and sign them to their labels. In March
2001, I flew back to Texas with Stevie Chick, my improbably named
music journalist friend, who was there to interview musicians

and review gigs for *NME*, a British music magazine. I was going to write a story for the travel pages of the *Standard*, and I'd arranged a free stay at the Barton Creek Resort, a swanky hotel, golf course, and conference center ten miles west of downtown, but when I got there it seemed far too remote and stuffy to serve as a base from which to write a story about America's live music capital. Instead, Stevie insisted I sleep on the sofa bed in his room at the Days Inn, a budget motel off I-35, a couple of miles north of downtown. In the car park were several Econoline vans used as tour buses, and in the breezeway outside Stevie's room, musicians hung out and smoked cigarettes, all dressed in denim with sunglasses. The Days Inn was the city in microcosm; there were bands everywhere, spilling out of doorways and drinking beer by the pool.

There was a kind of magic that pervaded the air during SXSW. If you could bear to roll out of bed before 10:00 A.M. and throw on some clothes, you might imagine a city still sleeping after a rough night on the tiles, but walk downtown and people were wandering around, bleary-eyed, clutching steaming coffees and eating breakfast tacos; bands were setting up to play morning shows on bar patios; and workers were cleaning up around them from the night before. By midday, you'd choose to walk on the shady side of the street to avoid the scorching sun, and your olfactory glands picked up the alternating scent of baked pavement and barbecue. As the day wore on, the music got louder and walking between venues was an unintelligible cacophony. In the spring of 2003, on the last night of my third consecutive SXSW festival, I met my future wife, Shannon, outside a club on Red River Street. We went for a drink in a nearby Irish bar (cosmopolitans, because she loved *Sex and the City*), and when I flew back to London the next day we promised to keep in touch.

Four years after discovering Austin for myself, I was now unequivocal: I'd find a way to move there. I'd wanted to call Austin home for a while, but after meeting Shannon I was even more determined. My attempts to persuade a couple of good friends from England to join me had failed miserably; it wasn't that they didn't want to, but one was a teacher and the other was a film editor, and it was all but impossible to get a visa that would allow them to find work. For me it was more straightforward: I'd apply for a media visa at the US consulate in London and make my living writing for the British press; the visa let me stay several years on the condition I didn't work for an American publication. Texas offered an unrivaled opportunity for a freelance journalist from England— I'd write about stuff that I never could back home: the death penalty, the US-Mexico border, apocalyptic religious movements. I knew I'd be more creatively stimulated in Austin. It felt like a place I could grow as a writer. I was smitten with the city—but also with this girl I'd randomly met on the street during a festival. That autumn I left my newspaper job in London and moved to Texas.

I thought Austin was the greatest city on earth. Rent was cheap (I paid $600 a month for a two-bedroom apartment a couple of miles east of downtown) and so was the food. I loved the heat; I loved the bars and the music. As much as I loved London, what I found in Austin was year-round sunny weather, better air quality, and ridiculously friendly people, all in a city that was easy to navigate. It was a place you could pitch up, find somewhere to live for cheap, get a job, make friends, and do something creative. The stereotype of the struggling artist on the balcony of her bohemian garret in Paris, sitting and smoking a cigarette, or the impoverished writer in his tiny New York City apartment, hammering away at the keyboard, turning his vision into a reality, exists for a reason: it's a potent emblem of the indomitable creative spirit. And that spirit was alive and well in Austin when I moved there, only there was a key difference: the apartments were bigger, living costs cheap, and the weather (so I thought back in 2003, anyway) was fabulous. Austin was affordable, and an affordable city tends to attract a more diverse population, which in turn leads to a richer mix of cultures, traditions, languages, and perspectives. An affordable city allows artists to pursue their creative passions, to take risks and innovate, without being overwhelmed by high living costs. Affordable cities see more community bonds, a sense of belonging and shared identity. In Austin you didn't need to struggle—you might only make a decent salary, but even so you could enjoy a fantastic quality of life.

For someone moving to Austin today, though, the opposite would be true. The demographic has changed so much that people who could afford to move there twenty years ago might not be able to. From 2003 to 2023 there's been an almost 300 percent increase in rent prices. You need to be earning around $135,000 in order to afford the principal, interest, taxes, and insurance payments on a median-priced home in Austin today. The average home price in the city of Austin proper was $670,000 in the summer of 2022, although it's declined since the pandemic; the median rent that same summer was $2,930. By the time I left, the city was no longer affordable for the bulk of people and certainly no longer a place that offered a refuge for artists and immigrants. The change in accessibility means that Austin is attracting a different kind of person, so the makeup of the city itself is changing based on who can afford to live there.

It reminds me of Detroit, which I first visited back in 2002 to write a story on the burgeoning garage rock music scene. Twenty years earlier its auto industry was like the Silicon Valley of its time, but the city's reliance on a single industry had come back to bite it when faced with rising production costs and global competition. When I got there, public school enrollment was declining, poverty was endemic, and the crime rate was rising. I wrote that the music scene, a triumph over adversity, was a "powerful force, set against the backdrop of a deserted but beautiful city peppered with incredible derelict suburban mansions, turn-of-the-century houses, and empty downtown office blocks." A decade later, musicians and artists from elsewhere, lured by cheap houses and the low cost of living, moved in. Today, though, the specter of displacement looms as surging real estate prices and development transform the city, leaving the working class struggling. I can't help but think about what happened to San Francisco and Detroit when looking at what's happened to Austin.

No one should be surprised by the changes underfoot in Austin today, because everything we're seeing now—families that have lived here for generations displaced by skyrocketing property taxes and cost of living; lack of affordable housing—has happened before. Everything was predictable. History is repeating itself. If we really wanted to stop that horse from bolting, we should have heeded those lessons of the past.

IN 1987, DOWELL MYERS, AN urban planning professor who had been based at the University of Texas, published a paper with the dry title "Internal Monitoring of Quality of Life for Economic Development." Myers's study was innovative in that he argued that quality of life is not just about objective measures such as income and crime rates, but also about how people feel about their lives and their communities. It focused on Austin and acknowledged what many Austinites instinctively knew—that music was instrumental to their quality of life—and he wrote that in the late 1970s and early '80s, Austin had explicitly promoted this and other qualities in order to lure high-tech firms to the city. Among Austin's "unique assets and amenities," which he identified in his study, were the state capital, the University of Texas, the laid-back lifestyle (which Myers concluded was "a product of student influence, summer heat, and a slower pace of activity"), an abundance of water resources for recreation, and the homegrown music scene.

In the late '70s, Austin was on the cusp of a tech boom. At the time, the most important of these businesses was the

Microelectronics and Computer Technology Corporation, or MCC. Persuading MCC to move to Austin in 1983 was a huge coup; before that, Austin's economic growth was due almost entirely to the University of Texas doubling its student body in just a decade to almost forty thousand by 1970 and to state government being one of the city's key employers. MCC's arrival represented a new tech strand to diversify Austin's economy. The city knew that winning the MCC prize would help give birth to a new Silicon Valley—MCC would be joining IBM, Motorola, and Texas Instruments, which had already made their homes there in the 1960s and early '70s, as well as homegrown companies that included CompuAdd Corporation and Dell in the early '80s. Austin was an attractive proposition, and the city lured these tech companies with tax incentives, rebates, and fee waivers in a state that already had zero state income tax. Although MCC would employ only around four hundred people, those backing the bid saw a potential gold mine of tech development following in its wake. A leading Austin real estate attorney named Ed Wendler Sr. said that after the successful MCC bid, speculators "came in here from Saudi Arabia, Canada, and God knows where, and started buying up the land."

Forrest Preece was born and bred in Austin; he can trace his lineage back to the cedar choppers, a clan of mountain folk who settled Appalachia in the 1700s before moving to Central Texas a century and a half later, eking out a living cutting ashe juniper for fencing and barns. Forrest was there as the wave that would ultimately shape the city's future began to gather momentum. After graduating from the University of Texas, he worked in marketing before starting his own ad agency, Good Right Arm, which he'd run for the next twenty-eight years. Forrest had the Dell Computer account until early 1987, by which time the company had gone from being a small operation run out of founder Michael Dell's dorm room to a $70 million business, and one that would become synonymous with Austin. It wasn't just Dell Computer that grew exponentially during that time. Forrest likens it to a "whale with a bunch of pilot fish around it. Michael Dell being here made a lot of ancillary companies spring up. People wanted to move to Texas for the weather, a whole stable of kids getting scientific or computer degrees each year from UT, and a sweet lifestyle. One time or another a lot of people worked for Dell, then went out on their own. It was like a starfish replicating itself."

Local developers anticipated the coming economic boom. Construction surged, with posh hotels, thousands of apartments, and office buildings springing up all over the city. In the decade up to 1990, office space grew from just under 6 million square feet to more than 20 million. Developers built subdivisions on the outskirts of town, including the million-square-foot Barton Creek Square Mall and the Arboretum mixed-use development. Austin was a boomtown, but the boom also caused casualties, and economic triumph would quickly threaten those very things that had made it such an attractive place to move to in the first place.

In his paper, Myers wrote that there was a real fear that development success "will kill the quality-of-life goose that lays the golden eggs." Sure enough, the MCC victory triggered a speculative boom that doubled land prices, resulting in a housing affordability crisis for the first time in the city's history. Myers's study found that until around 1980, Austin's average single-family home sales price had been running about $10,000 behind the national average, but thereafter, prices escalated to nearly $10,000 ahead of the national average, and by the middle of the decade, prospective workers were beginning to be turned off by the high cost of housing. And that wasn't all. There was traffic congestion, rampant construction threatened Austin's water quality and environment, and there were reports of the impending death of its renowned music scene. The surge in real estate prices was forcing some live music venues to close; others were torn down to make way for new offices.

One victim of Austin's skyrocketing property values was the fabled Armadillo World Headquarters, which was so intertwined with Austin's musical history. For some, this was the writing on the wall. In the summer of 1972, Willie Nelson had played a show at the Armadillo, an old National Guard armory on South First Street and Barton Springs Road that had been turned into a music venue, and gave birth to the "Austin sound"—a moment defined by hippies and rednecks uniting to enjoy a new style of country music, one that was inspired by rock and roll and infused with Austin's varied multicultural traditions. But less than a decade later the Armadillo, the very venue where the Austin sound was born, was replaced by a thirteen-story office building.

Next to fall was Soap Creek Saloon, one of the city's last big dance halls. An anecdote from the time that I think perfectly encapsulates how money trumped preserving the arts, even back in the 1980s, was that the company that declined to renew Soap Creek Saloon's license was owned by Willie Nelson. It was almost unbelievably ironic. There were other casualties too, of course. As well as Soap Creek, the country and western club the Silver Dollar was replaced by high-tech offices, and Xalapeno Charlie's was razed to build an industrial complex. Myers told me that when he first published his study, holding a press conference to announce the results, local TV stations in Austin ran it as their lead story on the six o'clock news, and the section about the decline in live music venues and nightclubs per capita "lit people up more than any other indicator."

Anyone following Austin's tech boom today, visible in the new steel and glass that dominate the skyline, will realize that you could easily replace the date "1987" at the top of Myers's study with the year you're reading this book. Big tech has once again consumed Austin, rents have soared, and venues have closed. Why does that matter? For one, the city still sells itself as the "Live Music Capital of the World." It's hard to quantify the exact number of music venues left in Austin today because the city has decided to change the definition of what a music venue actually is, which you might think is a little fishy. At the time of writing, the visitors bureau reckoned there were 219 venues, but its definition included any establishment that showcased live music regularly or "semi-regularly," and these included "retail shops, bars, restaurants, museums, grocery stores, record shops, outdoor spaces [and] hotels." Of the 219 music venues on its list, 52 weren't in Austin at all but in nearby towns. Troy Dillinger, who used to run Save Austin Music, a nonprofit trade organization that supports the city's music industry, is convinced it's simply inflating the number of venues. "If they didn't, they couldn't keep using the slogan 'Live Music Capital.' They have to justify it or they have to stop using it," he told me. "I guarantee there are less venues now." Troy reckons the city has changed the rules of the game so it can win it. He says that today any place that pushes two tables out of the way and puts a band in the corner can call itself a venue and the city will allow it.

"Live Music Capital of the World" was a marketing campaign—a pitch dreamed up by officials to promote Austin as a destination for tourists and businesses. The reason the city government and the chamber of commerce decided to champion it as a music destination in the first place could have been because that first tech boom that Dowell Myers examined back in the 1970s and early '80s threatened its very existence. To see it erased could spell commercial suicide, so perhaps unwilling to sit and watch Austin's music scene crumble before their eyes, they began an aggressive education campaign, promoting the city's musical heritage. Suddenly it was not just seen as a quality-of-life attraction to lure companies but as a potential new and exciting economic engine through tourism.

THE IDEA OF A CITY slogan had been echoing around Austin's streets for some time. The first was in 1976, a few years after Willie played that seminal gig at the Armadillo World Headquarters. Back then, Ernie Gammage, a local musician, told the chamber of commerce it was still publishing the same tired old brochure pushing the city's country music scene; country was great, Gammage said, but there was so much more to the Austin scene than that. The phrase "Live Music Capital of the World" first appeared in print in 1985, when the chamber took out a half-page ad in *Billboard* magazine to promote various homegrown bands, declaring the band's hometown as the gigging center of the globe. But what happened the following year would do more than help fulfill that prophecy.

In 1986, several Austin bands were invited to play the New Music Seminar, a music conference and festival that took place in New York City each June. Such was the buzz around Austin afterward that the convention organizers announced they were going to hold a satellite event in the Texas capital the following year; it would be called New Music Seminar Southwest. But a few months later they had a change of heart. Their sudden reticence upset two attendees just enough that they decided to launch a festival in Austin of their own. The story has become bound up in city legend: Roland Swenson, a nerdy music manager, together with his friend Louis Meyers, a music promoter, went back home to Austin and made a beeline for the offices of the city's alt-weekly newspaper the *Austin Chronicle,* where they pleaded with their friends Louis Black and Nick Barbaro, editor and publisher, respectively, to get on board. As Swenson put it: "We don't need New Yorkers. We can do this." Swenson persuaded the Convention and Visitors Bureau to part with five grand, and the South by Southwest festival was born. The first ever SXSW, in March 1987, lasted three days and saw 177 bands play fifteen clubs in town. A wristband cost ten dollars.

FOR THE FIRST TIME, IT felt like Austin could legitimately claim the crown as the country's live music capital. The year after SXSW launched, the city created the City of Austin Music Commission to help develop an industry it now saw as a cash cow. Nancy Coplin was its first chair. Sitting on the back porch of her house in south Austin, between sips of strong black coffee, she told me about the marketing campaign that Austin finally launched, sixteen years after Willie played his first gig at the Armadillo, to sell itself as a music city—a strategy so successful that it still exists to this day. Nancy came to Austin in the 1980s, began helping out with an organization that supported women business leaders in the community, and eventually got recommended for the inaugural Music Commission position. Friend and blues musician Lillian Stanfield suggested the phrase "Austin Texas Music Capital," which they figured could appear on signs at the city limits. It may seem like semantics, but ultimately the idea of "Music Capital" was discarded—too much competition with LA, New York, Nashville, and Chicago, they thought. Instead, they'd focus specifically on the number of music *venues* in the city, and after figuring that Austin had more per capita than anywhere else in the nation, "*Live* Music Capital of the World" stuck and was officially adopted by the City of Austin in 1991—although over the years several people have claimed to have invented the phrase. There was a rival bid from Branson, Missouri, for live music capital, but ultimately Branson dropped the "Live" and settled for "Music Capital of the World" instead, LA, New York, Nashville, and Chicago be damned.

THIS WASN'T LONG BEFORE I first came to town. When I got there I knew little of Austin's history, let alone the story behind "Live Music Capital of the World," and nothing of how the fortunes of the very things that made the city such an appealing

place to live, like its music scene, were inextricably tied to efforts
to bolster its tech economy. Less than a decade before I first laid
eyes on Austin, as the city was ramping up the publicity campaign around its music scene, the country at large was in the
throes of a financial crisis. Dowell Myers lived in Austin during
the city's economic expansion, and he was there when it came to
a crashing halt in the early 1990s.

The crash was in part due to the savings and loan industry,
which made billions in mortgage loans across the country to speculative real estate ventures, some of which were fraudulent, and
many too big for the institutions to handle. When interest rates
went up, the proverbial shit hit the fan, and nearly one in three
S&Ls failed, half of them in Texas, in what was the largest banking
collapse since the Great Depression. By the early 1990s, the United
States had plunged into a recession. The price of oil dropped, and
drilling and production in Texas slowed considerably. Austin, not
known as an oil city, suffered because many of its banks and investors backed the oil industry. At first the city's tech economy
looked like it would weather the storm, but not for long. In Austin,
according to Myers, real estate construction and investment had
oversaturated the market, and that, combined with a nationwide
downturn in the computer industry, had begun to impact the city.
The *Austin American-Statesman* newspaper said the outlook for local businesses in 1988 "ranged from lackluster to dismal," and the
chamber of commerce, acknowledging the growing vacant office
space, warned of a "painful and slow recovery process."

Ironically, the economic downturn may have been what helped
Austin's music scene recover; why when I sauntered through town
for the first time in 1999, it looked like that scene was as vibrant as I
could imagine. The saying goes that beer and liquor are recession-
proof, and in the early part of the new decade, music entrepreneurs
took advantage of vacant spaces and lower rents to open new clubs
and bars downtown. In *How to Kill a City*, their fascinating book

on gentrification, P. E. Moskowitz wrote that "every golden era" for culture and art in cities was possible "only because artists and activists were able to find cheap real estate in those cities." So, in the 1990s, as its economy tanked, artists and musicians flocked to Austin again. By the time I arrived at the end of the decade, Austin's economy was already on the upswing and it was palpable: the bars that had emerged a few years before were packed; music seeped onto the sidewalk from open doorways on Sixth Street.

IN MYERS'S STUDY ABOUT THE quality-of-life attributes Austin possessed that were so successful in enticing tech firms to the city, he also listed its abundance of water resources for recreation, which he said came under intensified threat once the big boom happened. I don't think this can be understated: Austin's natural springs, water holes, and rivers are one of the biggest reasons I fell for the city a little more than a decade later. But while I was swimming laps in the cold, refreshing waters of Barton Springs, the city's famous natural swimming hole a stone's throw from downtown, I was oblivious to the fact that this essential resource was at risk and had been for a long time. The Edwards Aquifer, a vast groundwater storage system that works symbiotically with the Colorado River to provide drinking water for two million people in Central Texas and is the main water source for the area's agriculture, also feeds the springs. It's an overtaxed and possibly even finite resource. Before I arrived in Austin, it hadn't rained for months on end; some Texas reservoirs were at their lowest levels since they were constructed three decades earlier. Ranchers sold off cattle as their pastures withered in the drought. People died from heat stroke. President Clinton declared Texas a disaster area, triggering millions in federal aid. In Austin, the Edwards Aquifer is recharged by rainwater, but it turns out more water was being pumped out of it than was seeping in. Math was never my strong suit, but even I could see that was unsustainable. And yet the city grows, and the weather gets drier and hotter.

MYERS ALSO TALKED ABOUT AUSTIN'S "summer heat" and "slower pace of activity" as key attractions. Back in 1999, I thought the weather was fantastic. Even when I experienced the tail end of my first Austin summer in 2003, when I moved to Texas from England, I loved the smell of ashe juniper trees baking in the sun and swimming in the warm waters of Lake Travis. I was oblivious to what was really going on: that climate change meant Austin's summers were getting hotter, those seasons stretching out for longer. And there would be consequences.

In 1878, John Wesley Powell, a geologist with an impressive beard, drew an invisible line running south to north from Mexico to Canada, splitting the United States into east and west. The line was called the 100th Meridian, and Powell warned against settling west of it. "On the east a luxuriant growth of grass is seen," he wrote, describing the prairie landscape as beautiful. Meanwhile, west of the line, "species after species of luxuriant grass and brilliant flowering plants disappear; the ground gradually becomes naked . . . now and then a thorny cactus is seen, and the yucca plant thrusts out its sharp bayonets." Of course, no one listened to Powell and the frontier pushed farther westward. After all, to paraphrase the Doors singer Jim Morrison, the West was the best.

Today, scientists have confirmed that the divide is very real, and Powell's line is gradually moving eastward because of climate change. Austin is on the wrong side of that line, destined to a future of aridity, with the western desert expanding eastward, or, as journalist Alan Neuhauser put it, "rushing toward the Louisiana border with each drought in a wave of tan and brown." More than one hundred people move to Austin each day. In 2020 alone, more than fifty thousand new residents called the city home. How many of them think that the water they drink, swim in, bathe in, or water their lawns with is an inevitability? Back in 1999, I had no idea that in a few years I'd be there to witness ninety triple-digit days in a single year—and the hottest day since records began—in a city I now called home too.

AUSTIN WAS CHOSEN AS THE Texas capital almost overnight on one man's whim. Mirabeau Lamar, the second president of the Republic of Texas, chose the site, then called Waterloo, for its beauty and potential, but not everyone was enthusiastic: newspaper editorials pointed out that the springs that he'd championed as a water source were unreliable and that the Colorado River was not navigable. Nevertheless, the city quickly emerged from the mesquite, oak, and cedar by the banks of the river.

By the late 1800s, a hydroelectric plant had been built to provide municipal electricity, but also to power prospective cotton mills, ensuring Austin would become the manufacturing center of the region, but the dam was structurally unsound. It failed during a rainstorm in 1900, flooding downtown Austin and killing fifty people. The City Beautiful movement—modern city planning with a focus on aesthetics and quality of life—inspired Austin officials to rebuild the dam, but this time with a focus on electricity generation for the city, cheaper water, as well as the creation of a downtown lake for recreation.

Austin wouldn't get its dam until 1940—its third attempt, after a second dam was abandoned owing to a dispute between the city and the contractor responsible. Finally, Austin had gone from a city whose government saw building a dam as pivotal in its quest to become the industrial capital of the South to one whose government saw that dam as a way to improve the city itself for the people who called it home. *That* was Austin's destiny—as a "City Beautiful." It's not a stretch to assume that had Austin not endured the tragedy of its dam collapsing in 1900, it would look very different today.

The lake in the middle of the city, where scores of Austinites take to canoes, kayaks, and paddleboards each weekend, would prove to be a remarkable asset. But back then, to some at least, water must have seemed like an infinite resource. Today its depletion threatens Austin's very existence, but it's not like we're only just now becoming aware of this. By the mid-1980s, the era Dowell Myers focused on for his study, more than 150 neighborhood groups comprising Austin residents mad at the rampant building boom and subsequent traffic congestion had sprung up to protest, and activists mobilized to form a powerful movement to protect Austin's natural environment and watersheds. Four decades later the population of Austin has gone from around 370,000 when those protests took place to a little under a million today. Austin is now the tenth largest city in America and its environment is under threat like never before.

There's a saying around here that the last day Austin was perfect was the day you moved to town. It's certainly true today, but it's been true pretty much since the city was founded: 140 years ago one writer lamented the razing of a two-story brick building built thirty years before as a jewelry store and residence. "Thus one by one the old landmarks leave us and but few of the original houses of Austin remain," he wrote. "A few years hence the citizen of thirty years ago will be a comparative stranger in the home of his youth with no familiar objects to greet his eye save the eternal hills on which the capitol city sits enthroned as a queen in her royal beauty and the sparkling Colorado at her feet." Perhaps the naysayers today are wearing rose-tinted glasses, lamenting the lost Austin of their youth. Get with the program, boomer, Austin's forever changing and maybe you've just outgrown it! Or perhaps something else is true. Perhaps the changes that Austin has undergone in the last two decades have been so profound, so expansive, that it's become a

place only the rich can afford to move to; and perhaps that spark—
that magic fairy dust that was sprinkled on the city by the very
folks who can no longer afford to call it home—has gone forever.

FOR OLDER AUSTINITES WHO HELPED cement its reputation
as a music city back in the day, what Austin has lost, as far as
they're concerned, is irretrievable. One morning I visited Marcia Ball and Gordon Fowler at their home on a corner lot in the
Zilker neighborhood. Marcia and Gordon are as close as you'll
get to Austin royalty: an inveterate raconteur, Gordon's a native
Texan who built his dad's small business, Wick Fowler's Two-
Alarm Chili, into a prominent national business; opened the La
Zona Rosa music venue on West Fourth and Rio Grande Streets
in the late 1980s with Marcia; and went on to become a notable
landscape painter. Marcia, meanwhile, is a five-time Grammy-
nominated blues singer and pianist whose car broke down in
Austin in 1970 while driving from Louisiana to California and
never left. Before she went solo, her band Freda and the Firedogs
was among the pioneers of Austin's progressive country movement. Between them, Marcia and Gordon have seen a lot of the
changes that have taken place here over the years.

We sat around their large dining table with one of Gordon's
portraits propped on a chair at the head, watching over us. Marcia
brewed coffee in a kitchen decorated with colorful Mexican tile,
and for the next couple of hours they tag-teamed tales of old Austin,
with Gordon interjecting witty asides and Marcia, gravelly voiced
and smiling, delivering the satisfying denouement. Marcia likes to
tell a story she heard once about someone's business partner who
was coming to Austin for a work meeting. "And he says, 'When I
get to Austin, how am I gonna find you?' And his colleague says,
'Well, when you get downtown, there are two tall buildings: there's
a gold one and a black one. I'm in the gold one.'" But that was then,

this is now, and that anecdote doesn't work today—not since the skyscraper-building boom began with the Frost Bank Tower, which Marcia affectionately refers to as "the nose-hair clippers." Today there are no longer two tall buildings. There are countless.

Gordon likes to recount something Eddie Wilson, cofounder of the Armadillo World Headquarters, always said: that people came to Austin for pretty girls, cold beer, and cheap pot. What do they come here for now? "Money, money, money," Gordon replied. "I was just saying to Marcia this morning, if we started eating at the new fancy restaurants that open up here by the day, we wouldn't live long enough to dine in them all, because they would be opening faster than we could get to 'em."

Back in the '80s, Marcia and Gordon were among the original band of locals fighting the developments that threatened Austin's natural areas—"Part of the Barton Springs posse," Gordon said.

"We fought every stick and every brick that was built between Barton Springs and Bee Cave," Marcia added. "We fought everything that they did, including the Barton Creek mall and MoPac and everything in between. And we never won anything—you can see that by the density of it."

Marcia wonders what really attracts people to Austin today, considering how much it's changed. What attracted her has long since faded. "It was a small city in the seventies—charming and idyllic—but with a big university and a state capitol and no dirty industry, full of liberal people," she said. "A lot of people came to school here and there were musicians among them, and they never left. There were just a lot of places to go hear music and there was a lot of music to hear." But as Austin grew, it became more expensive. "There were fewer clubs, and of course that's not the only thing that made this town attractive, but what I've had to come around to understanding is that we've moved over; we who made Austin what it was in the seventies and eighties are pretty damn irrelevant now. Today it's high tech and money, but they still love it, and they still come and they'll still say Austin's awesome." Yet she thinks that anyone not earning high wages in the tech industry must be struggling. It's almost impossible to work full-time as a musician and live in Austin today, she says, and she worries that it's unaffordable for schoolteachers and nurses too. Marcia stood up and walked back into the kitchen. "People who've lived in a neighborhood like ours their entire lives are being taxed out of their homes," she said. Marcia and Gordon wonder if one day the same thing will happen to them.

Meanwhile, the changes happening in Austin are visible from their front porch. Someone recently paid $1.8 million for the house across the street—"And they plan to remodel it too," she said. "That's what kills me about this neighborhood. These old thirteen-hundred-square-foot houses, three-bed one-baths, used to be enough. You raised your family in those. Now they pay that sort of money just to tear them down."

San Francisco, Denver, Seattle, Portland—all have experienced a surge in tech jobs and investment in recent years. And that surge has boosted their economies and arguably made these cities more attractive to young people. But it's also led to a rise in housing prices and rents, as well as a displacement of low-income residents from certain neighborhoods. In San Francisco the average home value rose 90 percent between 2009 and 2019, from $715,900 to $1.36 million. Gentrification has displaced low-income residents, made it more difficult for people to afford housing, and increased segregation, not to mention the fact it's led to a loss of cultural diversity. And in the case of Austin, at least, it all happened before. And we did nothing to stop it from happening all over again.

CHAPTER 2

SXSW

The SXSW festival has grown exponentially, to the degree that you could argue its growth is partly responsible for the city's explosion. It's certainly responsible for putting Austin on the map internationally. Back in 2001, my first festival, you could still drop into a club and catch the first twenty minutes of one act before hopping in a cab and scooting across town to see the last twenty minutes of another. Back then, SXSW wasn't really a festival aimed at music fans—it was a music industry conference where bands could get signed, although the organizers graciously sold wristbands to locals at a discount.

It was also a crazy, capricious riot of color and sound. From the back patio of Red Eyed Fly, Stevie Chick and I watched as a band called . . . And You Will Know Us by the Trail of Dead tipped over their amps, ripped down the lighting rig above the stage, and tore apart the plastic awning separating them from the street outside. They were just three songs in, and this was still our first night at SXSW, yet I'd just witnessed one of the most exciting, incendiary gigs I'd ever seen. The list of bands Stevie planned to see seemed far too long to check off in one week; for him, SXSW summed up everything he loved about discovering new music. The festival embodied, as he put it, "the revelation that you could just tumble down the road to the next venue and see something else wonderful," even though in some sense he thought it was a strange event for the music press to cover in that most of his readers couldn't experience it for themselves.

Back in 2001, at least, it felt quite exclusive. Each band we saw had something magical about them. There was Modey Lemon, a two-piece from Pittsburgh who wore identical white coveralls as they sweated their way through a fiery set of pure garage rock; Trachtenburg Family Slideshow Players—a dad, a mom, and their eight-year-old daughter on drums—who played delightful indie folk rock in front of a slideshow of photographs they'd found at garage sales and thrift stores; and Bobby Conn, a captivating, diminutive white Chicago singer in a single-color nylon tracksuit, who danced like James Brown and shifted from falsetto to baritone in perfect three-minute funk-pop numbers.

The following March we were back. That year Stevie watched Aaron North, a guitarist in the LA rock band the Icarus Line, pick up a mic stand mid-set and swing it into a glass case hanging on the wall next to the stage of the Hard Rock Cafe. In the case was a prize guitar that once belonged to Austin blues musician Stevie Ray Vaughan, who was a god in Texas. North grabbed the guitar by the neck, ripped it from the case, and ran to the back of the stage, apparently aiming to plug in and begin playing, but he never got the chance. Instead, several security guards leaped up and snatched the instrument from him. Stevie said it was one of the most rock and roll moments he'd ever witnessed. Everyone who goes to SXSW collects stories. It's been that way since the first festival back in 1987; it's exciting, unpredictable, intense, exhausting, and only one week in March. It's hard to imagine Austin looking any different when the festival is over, the heart of the city forever pumping with the sound of rock and roll.

Of course I knew that Austin wasn't like this all the time. A couple of months after meeting Shannon in 2003, I'd flown back to Austin for a visit and seen how quiet the city was post-festival. Its population was still swollen—by fifty thousand, mostly students, as the University of Texas was in session—but the sun-drenched downtown streets were silent during the day. If anything, this made the city more appealing. Thursday nights were when students took over the town, when bars ran drinks promotions; festival season—SXSW, Austin City Limits, which had launched the previous year, and Bat Fest, the year after I moved to town—was when hundreds of other people got to join the party; but for the rest of the year Austin was as laid-back a place as you could imagine.

When I relocated there full-time that September, between writing assignments, Shannon and I would meet friends at Pace Bend Park out on the lake, where we'd take turns launching ourselves into the cool water from the cliffs, or laze around in floats, chatting and drinking beer. By early evening we were back downtown picking up cheap Tex-Mex to eat at my condo, barhopping on Sixth Street, or watching alt-country shows at the Continental Club. Days bled into one another. Mornings began with rocket fuel coffee from quirky cafés. Shannon would go off to college, and I'd sit down to write or hop in an old Ford Contour I'd picked up for a few thousand bucks and drive off to do an interview. By midafternoon we'd join our friends at the lake and stay until the sky turned orange. Rinse. Repeat. It was a lifestyle I'd never have imagined living back in London. I felt massively privileged to call Austin home, but I was deliriously oblivious to the drumbeat of change getting louder by the day.

WHAT I DIDN'T KNOW WHEN I moved there, telling anyone who'd listen that I now lived in the "Live Music Capital of the World," was that some of those bands weren't happy about what SXSW was becoming. Originally from New England, Will Sheff, a musician with a red beard and a sweep of dark hair, moved to Austin in 1998 to start a band with some friends after finishing college in St. Paul, Minnesota. They rented a house near the university; Will's room served as the rehearsal space, and during the day he'd push his air mattress up against the wall to make room for the band to play. Austin was, he told me, "a repository for freaks in Texas: musicians, weirdos, an interesting mix of intellectuals and cowboys, drug adventurers, libertarians, and hippies." It was a time, he said, when . . . And You Will Know Us by the Trail of Dead had blown up, he would regularly see Britt Daniel, the lead singer of Spoon, around town, and Richard Linklater and Robert Rodriguez were making movies in the city. "Everybody was like, 'Wow, Texas is really cool and exciting.' And we thought, *Damn right, Austin fucking rules*." Will had split up with a girlfriend after she moved to New York, and he says he had a chip on his shoulder about the East Coast and took a dim view of its music scene. It was in this climate that he started his band Okkervil River.

Okkervil River played SXSW several times in the early 2000s, but Will quickly became jaded with a festival at which, so the conventional wisdom went, bands would get signed, find management, or secure publishing deals. "It just became overrun with coked-out publicists and people who didn't even want to see shows," Will told me. "They'd just come to throw up green beer on Sixth Street for St. Patrick's Day. I don't know if there's a single musician in the entire world who thinks that SXSW is a good place to make art who has actually been there. I mean, I have talked to musicians from outside of America who dream of playing SXSW, but when you actually do it, you realize this is the worst possible environment to play a show. I've had to fight with somebody to park the van, and I'm playing for a bunch of people drunk on fucking free Crystal Head Vodka, staring at their phones and talking. And they're music business people who already are burned out and jaded about music. And this is, like, the twentieth show the person mixing my sound has done today and their ears are fried. They're mad at me. They're mad at themselves for taking this fucking job. I'm sweating my ass off, and I can't hear myself because chances are I didn't even get a fucking sound check and so it probably sounds like shit. And nobody cares."

From my vantage point, I was totally unaware of any controversy. I was too busy getting obliterated and enjoying the show. One thing particularly grated at Will: clearly *someone* was making a lot of money from SXSW, and it wasn't the bands. But more than that, he started to see the festival as part of a wider problem: that people had begun to "bottle" what he called "the beautiful spirit of Austin" and market it for their own gain, to "treat it like a natural resource and take all the money for themselves." One year, after playing what he reckoned was ten shows during the festival, Will felt like he was run ragged and decided to treat himself to a meal at Vespaio, a nice Italian restaurant on South Congress Avenue. Midway through his meal he got up to use the bathroom and noticed Louis Black, one of the festival's founders and an Austin institution, sitting in a corner of the restaurant with a group of men who, Will said, looked like a bunch of wiseguys. "It was like fucking *Goodfellas*. And in my mind he was spanning out a gigantic stack of cash. He wasn't, of course, but that was very much the feeling."

By the mid-2000s, SXSW was becoming less of a festival for unsigned bands to demonstrate their mettle to record labels and more of a party for music lovers. In truth, the change was instigated by the musicians themselves. Many, tired of playing to suits, began to play free daytime shows around the city, much to the irritation of festival organizers. How could they justify a several-hundred-dollar price tag for a platinum pass ($1,675 today) if the same bands that executives were paying to see were playing free gigs in record stores, cafés, and impromptu pop-up stages all over Austin? They didn't admit that, of course. Publicly they said it was simply a liability issue—if these unofficial venues used the term "SXSW" in their advertising, could the festival be sued if something went wrong? Some, though, saw the growth of SXSW as just another layer adding to the commodification of Austin, and they reckoned it came at the expense of the very musicians it was supposed to be championing.

Jeff Klein moved to Austin in 1999, the same year I first got there. As a solo artist, Jeff was signed to One Little Indian (now One Little Independent Records), although he'd become better known for his band My Jerusalem. Jeff reckons he's played SXSW sixteen times, and each time he said friends would come to the city to join him for the festival and at the end of the week want to move there. Yet each time he'd tell them: this was absolutely not what it was like any other time of the year. Like a lot of bands, Jeff would also ignore the "rules" and play unofficial shows because they often paid good money. He heard one band got fifteen grand to play a corporate party, and he blames SXSW for creating the "perfect environment" in which musicians *could* profit, except they weren't allowed to. "The heartbreaking thing is," he told me, "friends' bands would come to Austin, and they'd tell me they were spending two grand getting here from Detroit to stay for a week, and I'd say, 'Do not spend two grand to come down and play for thirty minutes on a Wednesday at seven P.M. when you're up against all these other huge acts.'"

FROM THE FRONT ROW, THOUGH, you wouldn't notice anything amiss. I certainly didn't. The fact that it was getting bigger felt, in many ways, like progress, or like validation of the city's tremendous appeal. And while these changes felt, to me, positive, the festival's growth signaled how Austin was growing too. After all, with any boom or bust comes change; the fate of Austin's live music scene was becoming steadily more intertwined with the fortunes of its tech industry and the influx of people attracted to its well-paid jobs. Like many others, I enjoyed the music of SXSW, not knowing that the next tech boom would again prove to be a devastating blow for Austin's venues.

Over the years I'd call Austin home, SXSW would transform into a giant beast of a festival, with major artists like Ice Cube, R.E.M., Van Morrison, and Metallica playing where unsigned hopefuls used to tread. In 2009, a denim-clad Kanye West appeared onstage in a vast tent erected near I-35 sponsored by Levi's. In December 2011, after almost twenty years sitting on the corner of Sixth and Red River Streets, Emo's, a beacon of the '90s Austin punk scene and a stalwart SXSW venue, would shut its doors, moving to a shiny new location on East Riverside Drive. Sterile and now no different from a thousand other venues, the new Emo's was too far away to include on a drunken barhop downtown any longer. And you wouldn't want to, anyway. It just wasn't the same. That same year, Momo's closed too. Shutting so soon after Emo's was, to longtime Austinites, further proof that development downtown was forcing the city to reassess its commitment to live music. By 2012, according to local journalist Joe Nick Patoski, SXSW had become the highest-revenue-producing event for Austin's economy. "Seventy-five dollar parking in lots downtown during the peak of SXSW became the going rate—if you could find a space," he noted. Then there was the gratuitous branding. By 2014, Lady Gaga would perform on a stage designed to resemble a sixty-foot-tall Doritos vending machine.

Some people began to wonder: Could SXSW reclaim its soul? Andrea Swensson (no relation to SXSW founder Roland Swenson), a music journalist writing for NPR, said that after six consecutive years attending the festival, she'd finally given up on it for good. "I can't help but feel that it has strayed far away from its original premise as a grassroots gathering place for new, undiscovered talent and increasingly feels like a big ol'

Times Square billboard-sized commercial," she wrote, adding, "But the rampant expansion I've witnessed over the last handful of years feels too glaring and incongruous to ignore."

During the same 2014 festival that featured the Doritos stage, a man plowed his car into attendees downtown, killing four of them. He was drunk, trying to escape from the cops, and was eventually found guilty and sentenced to life in prison. But afterward, the voices calling for SXSW organizers to look seriously at the festival's impact on the city grew louder. Even the usually deferential local Austin press was concerned. An op-ed in the *Statesman* compared the growth of SXSW with that of Utah's Sundance Film Festival, quoting its cofounder Robert Redford as saying, "As [Sundance] grew, so did the crowds, so did the development in Park City. Well, at some point, if both those things continue to grow, they're going to begin to choke each other." Gissela SantaCruz, author of that *Statesman* op-ed, asked, "When it comes to public events, is bigger always better?" She concluded that what began in 1987 as a stage to showcase independent musicians—adding film and interactive branches to the festival a few years later—had now exploded into one of the state's biggest spring break gatherings, "full of big names, big parties and bigger headaches for those who live and work in downtown where most of the official and unofficial SXSW gigs take place."

BUT THAT WAS ALL IN the future. Back in 2003, when I moved from London to Austin, the boom was only just beginning.

CHAPTER 3

BOOM

Austin officially became a "weird" city the year after I first visited. In 2000, a librarian, Red Wassenich, called in to a local radio station to donate to its funding drive live on air. When Red was asked why he was giving money, he replied, "It helps keep Austin weird." In the intervening years, while Wassenich had multiple opportunities to profit from the phrase, he decided not to trademark it. When he died in 2020, a family friend told the *Austin Chronicle* he'd always believed that commercializing it was "the antithesis of weird." Even people who have never been to the city are familiar with Red's phrase, even if they've never heard of Red himself. And they naturally think that Austin must be a weird city.

AUSTIN FELT LIKE A BREEDING ground for eccentrics—or as musician Jeff Klein described them to me, "such beautiful weirdos." There was Roky Erickson, founding member of Austin psychedelic rock pioneers the 13th Floor Elevators. Record producer Bill Bentley once recalled there was something about Erickson's band that went beyond music—mainly, he said, "because they were on LSD almost every time they played." Diagnosed with paranoid schizophrenia, Erickson spent time in a psychiatric hospital. After he got out, he received electroconvulsive shock therapy after speaking gibberish while performing. A year later he was picked up for marijuana possession and, because this was Texas, faced a decade in prison for having just one joint. His only option to avoid an outlandish sentence was to claim insanity, which meant more psychiatric hospitals. Then there was Daniel Johnston, a beloved Austin singer-songwriter and artist known for his lo-fi, home-taped recordings and personal lyrics. Johnston painted a huge, childlike mural of a frog on a brick wall near the University of Texas campus with the words "Hi, How Are You" and watched, several years later, as the entire city united to protect it when a new store owner wanted to paint over it. And there was Leslie Cochran, the true icon of the "Keep Austin Weird" movement. Known for his flamboyant fashion sense, which usually amounted to a thong, feather boa, and tiara, Cochran, who was homeless, became a fixture on Austin's downtown streets, embodying the unconventional spirit of the city, and ran for mayor three times. Austin loved its free spirits. Remember how Dowell Myers wrote in his study that the tech boom of the late '70s and early '80s risked killing the quality-of-life factor that made Austin such a compelling home for creatives? Well, the next boom was coming for its beautiful weirdos.

Ironically, one particular eccentric Austinite helped pave the way for that next big tech boom. Richard Garriott made his fortune developing computer games in the 1980s, but I wonder whether it could have ever happened anywhere except Austin. Austin embraced people like Richard. I first met him at his mansion overlooking Lake Travis. Born in England, his gaming name was Lord British, and he called his home Britannia Manor, although it was unlike anything I'd ever seen back home. There were suits of armor standing guard at an elaborate portico entrance, and Richard was like an excited child showing off his Christmas gifts as he took me on a tour of the house: the inside-outside swimming pool, the secret passageways and rooms, a cannon near the entrance, and a working observatory. He'd paid $30 million to spend twelve days aboard the International Space Station, taken a submersible seven miles to the bottom of the sea to look at the Mariana Trench, and collected shrunken human heads, ancient fossils, bits of meteorite, and various other strange things.

Although he'd grown up in Houston, Richard fell in love with Austin after attending the University of Texas in 1979; it was far more his speed: outdoorsy, beautiful, with an eclectic mix of people. UT was the antithesis of his high school back east: here the nerds didn't get picked on by the jocks. Cliques existed, but everyone seemed happy mixing, and Richard liked the fact that uniqueness was celebrated. While he was at college he'd developed a series of fantasy role-playing games called *Ultima*, originally released for the Apple II computer. By the time he'd written *Ultima III*, his brother, Robert, a business school graduate, suggested they form their own company, and in 1983, Origin Systems was born. In Austin, the Garriott brothers saw a city brimming with opportunity. These were the days when the job of "computer artist" had barely entered the lexicon, and very few people were actually designing games for a living. Austin did have a rock and roll poster industry, though, which had emerged from the psychedelic music scene of the 1960s, so the Garriotts hired pen and ink illustrators more accustomed to drawing posters for 13th Floor Elevators gigs at the Armadillo World Headquarters than working on computer games. In 1992, less than a decade after they'd launched their company, Richard and Robert sold Origin to Electronic Arts for $35 million. Ten years on, their second computer business, Destination Games, was acquired by the Korea-based gaming company NCSoft.

By the early 2000s, Austin had its own gaming conference to rival San Francisco's and was on its way to becoming the online gaming capital of the United States, helping usher in the next wave of tech to the city. Firms like IBM and Sematech were already firmly entrenched, but they existed in a different world from the one the Garriotts inhabited. Gaming was still seen as an oddball cult class of the tech industry. But it was an oddball cult class that was growing bigger.

In Austin, talent was affordable; people were migrating there because it was attractive and inexpensive, and they could make a living pursuing their passions and dreams. Back then it felt like a manageable city just shy of seven hundred thousand people. But the new tech juggernaut was gaining steam, and Richard Garriott was going to be its poster child. An astrologist writing in the *Statesman* predicted that more huge, high-tech companies would move to the city. "Austin will continue to grow," she surmised, peering deep into her crystal ball, "and that will cause problems."

IT MAY NOT HAVE BEEN immediately palpable, but the energy of the Austin that nurtured Richard Garriott's ambitions to start a quirky computer game company—that same spirit that had embraced Leslie Cochran, celebrated Roky Erickson, and applauded Daniel Johnston—had already begun to shift. By the mid-2000s, developers, their financiers, and city planners in Texas had Austin in their sights for major redevelopment projects. Disused warehouses and office buildings suddenly became hot real estate propositions to convert into accommodation. Before too long the center of Austin would feel like a European city with alfresco dining and an outdoor café culture, but when I moved there in 2003 the only life downtown was at rush hour on weekdays in the few blocks surrounding the capitol. Thursday, Friday, and Saturday nights were busy with late-night partygoers out on Sixth Street. But other than that, save for the grackles ca-cawing in the sidewalk trees, Austin was a fairly quiet place. Yet behind the scenes, a seismic shift was taking place.

Venture capital investment in Austin companies had risen more than 20 percent. The City of Austin was also touting its planned redevelopment of the old Mueller airport site, which it promised would be transformed into a live-work suburban mecca that included a hospital, homes, shops, and restaurants. Rent was the lowest it had been in seven years. March 2004 saw SXSW and a handful of other big events inject some $60 million into the city's economy, and the mood was buoyant. As developers illuminated the top of Austin's new tallest building, the Frost Bank Tower, a 515-foot futuristic skyscraper clad in silver and glass (those "nose-hair clippers," according to Marcia Ball), Tim Hendricks, a senior vice president for the tower's developer, said he saw it as a symbol of Austin for the next hundred years. But Hendricks had spoken too soon. In just four years a new condo would usurp Frost Bank Tower as the city's tallest; developers were about to out-develop developers, and Austin's skyline was about to change forever.

OVER THE NEXT FEW YEARS Austin would have one of the fastest-growing job markets in the country, and sure enough, by the fall of 2004, apartments were at 90 percent occupancy. By early 2005, investors from California flocked to Texas to snap up single-family homes for as little as $60 per square foot (by comparison, in Brooklyn around the same time, the median price per square foot was $320 for town houses and $343 for condos and co-ops). Freescale Semiconductor Inc. announced it had chosen Austin over Chicago for its corporate headquarters, lured by a package of incentives worth around $30 million. Candidates vying for a spot on the city council, however, warned the Freescale deal would inevitably lead to high taxes and traffic problems and undermine small businesses. Tax breaks, they said, should be going to small Austin companies, not to corporate behemoths. But it was like nobody was listening. Austin's Planning Commission was considering a proposal for a thirty-six-story condo tower called Spring on the western edge of town, but current limits capped buildings at ten stories. A month later, Spring got the go-ahead anyway; despite opposition from residents to skyscrapers dominating their neighborhoods, the city insisted there was no better place for density than downtown. When it was completed in 2009, Spring became the third-tallest building in Austin. In 2006, wooed by $200 million of incentives, Samsung chose Austin for its new $3.5 billion chip manufacturing plant—a 1.6-million-square-foot building that would make it the largest single semiconductor facility in the country.

At the dawn of 2007, Austin was fresh from a record year for home sales, and unemployment was at its lowest in almost six years. But the nationwide housing bubble was about to burst, and the country would plunge into the worst recession since the Great Depression, caused largely by the failure to regulate the financial industry and curb subprime lending. For a while it looked like Texas might be immune to what was going on elsewhere, but there were signs things had begun to slow down. In Austin, thousands of people stood gawking as the $124 million Intel Corporation building on West Fifth Street, abandoned by the computer giant in the economic downturn, was destroyed in a controlled implosion. In 2008, the number of home sales plunged to the lowest in more than a decade; the Austin economy may have hit the pause button, but it never nosedived.

ASKING SOMEONE LIKE RICHARD GARRIOTT, Matthew Mc-Conaughey, or any other ultra-wealthy Austinite what they think of the city today—if they lament the rapid growth and the irreversible changes that have taken place—is redundant. When you're worth millions or billions of dollars, it's fair to assume you're not all that aware of a rise in the price of groceries or your electric bill; you can remain gloriously oblivious to the sea changes or even about what your presence and that of other wealthy people like you means for people with far less money. I'm not suggesting these people don't care what's happened to Austin, just that they probably haven't noticed. Richard may be eccentric, but he embodies a new kind of eccentricity that has come to Austin. Most of Austin's weirdos over the years have been artists and musicians and slackers who didn't have a lot of money, if any, but who could be who they wanted in a city that embraced them and that was cheap enough to survive and even thrive in. Most of today's weirdos, if they can even be called that, have the economic means to call Austin home.

Whenever it was that I first encountered Leslie Cochran, he was wearing a pink bra and knickers and holding court, probably to a group of drunk students or out-of-towners. It was easy to write Leslie off as an entertaining eccentricity who was (mostly) beloved by Austinites. But I was equally interested in his homemade rickshaw parked on a nearby curb—a gigantic wooden box constructed around a three-wheeled bicycle. Inside were Leslie's possessions, but on the outside of the box, he'd written a screed against the treatment of homeless people in Austin by the police. In 2000, his anger at that treatment prompted a run for mayor. He came in second with almost 8 percent of the vote. He ran again (unsuccessfully) in 2003. Leslie moved to Austin in 1996, but instead of reforms aimed at helping people like him, the city instead passed legislation to outlaw camping on the streets with the aim to make downtown more attractive to businesses. Leslie died in 2012—his health had declined after suffering a head injury that doctors suspected was due to a fall after having a stroke. An obituary in the *New York Times* reckoned that his passing presaged a changing Austin, that the city was in "danger of losing the simple, quirky vibe that made it special in the first place." Three years after Leslie's death, an association of business owners dedicated to preserving the Sixth Street Historic District unveiled a historic plaque celebrating his life and the contributions he made to the area. "Leslie, Queen of Austin (born Albert Leslie Cochran)," it read, "roamed 6th St. in g-strings and heels with his trademark goatee . . . A political activist, he ran for mayor 3 times, coming in 2nd place once . . . He embodied the 'Keep Austin Weird' spirit, inspiring dress-up refrigerator magnets and the iLeslie phone app with soundbites and interviews."

So yes, it's true that a cross-dressing homeless man once ran for mayor three times. And it's true that every Sunday between 4:00 and 8:00 P.M. at the Little Longhorn Saloon you can still place your bets on which bingo numbers a chicken sitting on a platform above the table will shit on between the grilles (it's called "chicken shit bingo" for a reason). And we always saw some shirtless, thong-wearing guy cycling around downtown with a cat on his shoulder, but I don't believe Austin has ever really been a weird city—just that it was, at least until recently, affordable enough for some really eccentric people to live there. People like Leslie could call it home and for the most part feel accepted there. Now they're lost amid the skyscrapers vying for pole position as the tallest in a city becoming defined by them.

A friend once told me Austin reminded her of the Island of Misfit Toys in the 1964 stop-motion TV special *Rudolph the Red-Nosed Reindeer*. In it, Rudolph and his friends Hermey, a maverick elf who leaves Santa's workshop to become a dentist, and Yukon Cornelius, a failed gold prospector, all travel to an island full of unwanted or unloved toys. Austin attracts people who want to do something outside the box, people who want to remain misfits and not be ostracized for being different. Today, as the city has grown, the misfits have largely left the building. Meanwhile, Austin has also been home to a darker kind of crazy—and unfortunately, some of it has stuck around.

CHAPTER 4

LIBERTARIAN CITY

The summer before I moved to America, I went to a backyard barbecue at a friend's house in south London. We'd worked together on the features desk of the *Evening Standard,* where I'd spent most of the last few years writing about arts and music, and she'd invited our former boss, who, between bites of a burger, informed me that once I moved to Texas, death row and the religious right would be my bread and butter. A month after landing in the United States, her prediction came true. In fact, anything that illustrated how Americans and the British were two cultures separated by a common language seemed to land with editors back home: gun culture, executions, the border. Stories about ordinary people doing extraordinary things were everywhere, but what was different for a British journalist working in America was access. People were willing—eager, even—to talk. In Texas especially, there was no shortage of these stories to cover, and that made my job a whole lot easier.

RICHARD LINKLATER'S MOVIE *SLACKER* CAME out in 1990 and managed to perfectly capture Austin at a moment in time. It follows a ragtag bunch of misfits over the course of one day as they opt out of mainstream society. There are the philosophical grad students who pontificate over coffee and pastries, the hipster attempting to sell what she insists is Madonna's pap smear, and a conspiracy peddler who clutches a tall glass of iced coffee as he tags along with a student clearly uninterested in his ramblings. The space program, he tells him, was a giant cover-up between the United States and the Soviet Union: "We've been on the moon since the 1950s . . . We've been on Mars since '62." Just before the student ditches him by slipping into a friend's house, the man tells him: "I'm just gonna stick around outside just for a little while, you know, and kinda make sure everything's okay, you know, make sure we weren't followed." *Slacker* is like a stitched-together series of monologues by disaffected, oddball characters who encapsulated a subset of Austinites in the 1990s. It's also pretty accurate at depicting these "types." "Texas," an old man says, "so full of these so-called modern-day libertarians with all their goddamn selfish individualism. Just the opposite of real anarchism; they don't give a damn about improving the world . . . This town has always had its share of crazies."

I would see those same philosophical grad students in coffee shops around town. I was served coffee by a bearded PhD student who once told me he couldn't find a well-paid job but that he didn't want to leave Austin; he'd swap a job in corporate America for a city he loved any day. I'd also met my fair share of conspiracy theorists who believed in chemtrails; gun hoarders; and antigovernment types. Austin was a magnet for quirky, paranoid people obsessed with nonexistent secretive plots—fans of the "slippery slope" argument, which goes something like this: if government is allowed to take a modest step today, that step will be far less modest tomorrow. And on the third day, well, you can forget about your freedoms altogether. Austinites weren't like East or West Coast liberals. They were something else entirely—culturally progressive, yes, but of a libertarian persuasion with a heap of neoliberalism thrown in for good measure. They were pro–gay marriage, yet quite liked the idea of keeping a Glock 9mm for protection beside their beds. The city was imbued with, as the academic James Rushing Daniel wrote, "a unique form of leftism inflected by anarchist and libertarian sentiments"—a brand of politics that would only become more amplified when Joe Rogan and Elon Musk moved to town.

Libertarians—or perhaps more accurately extreme libertarians—harbor an irrational fear that they are being targeted by the government, and I found that kind of thinking surfacing more often than I expected in Austin. In the '90s, when *Slacker* was set, the city's local public access television was inhabited by these people, fronting a seemingly endless number of bizarre, weird, or religious shows. One of the hosts of those programs was Alex Jones.

Plump, with a round face and short brown hair combed over to one side, Jones would usually opt for an open-collared shirt and blazer on camera—you know, that professional, authoritative look—and, sitting behind a desk, he'd gesticulate wildly with one hand while shuffling papers with the other as he became ever more animated by whatever topic of the day he'd chosen to be irate about. Despite his comical persona, Jones's growing legion of fans paid attention to him. He was Austin's most famous conspiracy theorist, and by the time *Slacker* came out he was already a fairly well-known figure in the city. Ten years later he walked into an audition for Linklater's animated feature film *Waking Life*. Linklater was well aware who Jones was. "He was this hyper guy that we'd all kind of make fun of," he once said. In *Waking Life*, Linklater painted a character that played up to those stereotypes. Jones drives around Austin with a megaphone attached to the roof of his car, ranting that the "corporate slave state" is conditioning us all "so we'll willingly give up our sovereignty, our liberty, our destiny ... on a mass scale." Jones's character was just an oddball eccentric, a quirky and seemingly harmless addition to Austin's eclectic mix of residents, but in reality he was capable of rallying the extreme libertarian troops—and he was about to project his rants on a much bigger stage.

BY THE TIME *WAKING LIFE* came out, Jones had launched Infowars, a website devoted to his elaborate, conspiratorial diatribes and fake news. Soon, I'd notice Infowars stickers plastered all over town—on mailboxes and streetlights, along Austin's hike-and-bike trails, and on the walls of public bathrooms. Some of what Jones said on his show was fairly innocuous, amusing even; other monologues were clearly intentionally provocative and offensive: we were experiencing a "New World Order" overseen by an ancient cabal of evil elites (an anti-Semitic trope); Lady Gaga's Super Bowl halftime show was in fact a satanic ritual; when the US government wasn't controlling the weather with radioactive isotopes it was secretively adding to jet fuel, it was attempting to turn kids gay with a chemical lining that it put in juice boxes. Jones also believed the US government was involved in the 1995 Oklahoma City bombing and that 9/11 was an inside job. I interviewed him for a story I was writing about the anniversary of the Waco siege—the fifty-one-day standoff between FBI agents and members of the Branch Davidian religious sect that took place in 1993 in Waco, Texas, one hundred miles north of Austin—which ended when, according to the FBI, the Davidians burned the compound to the ground. In all, seventy-five men, women, and children died. Waco had made a massive impression on Jones, then a high school senior in Austin, inspiring him to launch his career on public access television. In the aftermath, he had spearheaded a campaign to rebuild the Branch Davidian church.

Jones was furious at the government's botched handling of the incident, and a lot of what he told me seemed to mirror the consensus among the general public. "It happened so close to Austin where I live and I had a bad feeling about the whole thing," he told me. "A bunch of tanks, and churches blowing up, and huge orange mushroom fireballs . . . And I said let's build them a chapel." The story of the Waco siege and its aftermath—

agents of a powerful government pitted against Bible-believing churchgoers—fit Jones's schtick perfectly. And the weird thing was at first he actually came across as fairly sane when discussing it. But it didn't take long for him to plunge down the rabbit hole into conspiracyville. "We fundamentally understand [Waco] was meant to demonize gun owners," he said. "And it absolutely backfired on the establishment when they torched those people and barbecued them. And so a lot of gun owners, a lot of militia people, a lot of people that understand the danger of too-big government, resonate with the Branch Davidians." Jones believed there were army manuals that trained soldiers in gun confiscation techniques, teaching them to lock down entire US cities and go door-to-door taking weapons. "You need to understand this is not a delusion," he said. "This is a moment in history we're at where the federal government are going ahead and trying to start a civil war in this country—a civil war I don't want to happen." Jones insisted he wasn't calling for armed resistance, but he was convinced it was imminent. "You better believe it," he said.

Austin has a reputation for being open-minded and hosting a variety of alternative viewpoints, and Jones's presence might have, initially at least, contributed to the city's diverse landscape of ideas, even if some of those ideas were considered fringe or extreme by some. But while Austin may be swimming in free speech, in an unmoderated ocean where you can pretty much say and think whatever you want, you'll sooner or later end up with the bad thrown in with the good. Alex Jones's Infowars was ripe for the internet age, and in the early 2000s, his star began to rise among a growing legion of conspiracy buffs. With the birth of Facebook in 2004 and Twitter a few years later, he amassed an astonishing number of followers. By the time those social networks permanently suspended both Infowars and Alex Jones (Twitter in 2018, Facebook a year later), he had nearly four million followers across his accounts. As one writer friend in Austin told me: "Austin has this openness—which means it's also open to crazies. And we live side by side with them. But in the 1980s, Alex Jones was a clown. I didn't think he'd be sharing a stage with the president in a few years."

Long before he courted Donald Trump, though, he had become an inspiration to other antigovernment extremists. In April 2009, a twenty-two-year-old man shot and killed three police officers in Pittsburgh who were responding to a domestic dispute. Richard Poplawski, who reporters said had posted on Jones's Infowars website, believed a secret cabal of Jews ran the United States and that US troops were about to confiscate guns from ordinary Americans like him. Then in 2012, two weeks before Christmas, twenty-year-old Adam Lanza woke up, shot his mother in the head four times while she lay in bed, then drove five miles to Sandy Hook Elementary School in Newtown, Connecticut, where he shot and killed twenty young children and six staff members before turning the gun on himself. At first, Jones's "take" was that the mainstream media encouraged deranged people to target schools because it liked to hype shootings—all with the express intention of ultimately disarming Americans. He predicted that then president Barack Obama would use the Sandy Hook shooting to call for more gun control. But pretty soon he started to say something far more troubling: that the Sandy Hook massacre had been staged, that the victims were "crisis actors," and that, actually, it was a false flag operation and no one at all had died that day. Jones had gone from a circus sideshow to something far more sinister.

A few years later, in the run-up to the 2016 presidential election, Jones helped promote a Far Right conspiracy theory that became known as "Pizzagate." Days before the election, James Alefantis, the owner of a Washington, D.C., pizzeria, discovered that his Instagram account was being bombarded with comments calling him a pedophile. Weeks earlier WikiLeaks had released a tranche of hacked emails from Hillary Clinton's campaign chair,

John Podesta. In one of those messages, Alefantis had discussed with Podesta a possible fundraiser at his pizzeria, Comet Ping Pong; in another, Podesta had specified "cheese pizza." Meanwhile, somewhere buried deep within the endless threads that constitute right-wing internet message boards, somebody had given birth to an intricate conspiracy: anonymous users convinced themselves that "cheese pizza" was code for "child pornography" and indulged a fantasy that Comet Ping Pong was ground zero of a huge Democratic Party child sex ring. At the time, it was easy to laugh off Pizzagate as the fanatical rantings of a tiny minority of unhinged Infowars fans. But shortly after the election, a twenty-eight-year-old warehouse worker from North Carolina left his home at sunrise and began the 350-mile journey to the nation's capital. Edgar Maddison Welch pulled up outside Comet Ping Pong, then walked inside with a revolver and a loaded AR-15 assault rifle and opened fire. Incredibly, nobody was hurt or killed, and Welch was eventually sentenced to four years in prison, but it proved that words mattered. During an appearance on Infowars a year before he became president, Trump told Jones, "Your reputation is amazing. I will not let you down." In response, Jones said 90 percent of his audience supported Trump's candidacy. With the election of Trump, Alex Jones became emboldened. It was a match made in hell.

Even for those who'd previously viewed him as a harmless laughingstock, Jones was clearly toxic property. It was impossible to laugh at him any longer after witnessing the horrible acts he spurred on. The parents of Sandy Hook victims took him to court, contending that his public proclamations that the shooting was staged compounded their distress. In 2022, the courts ordered him to pay just under $1.5 billion to those families for spreading conspiracy theories that resulted in harassment. One of Austin's most famous exports was now persona non grata. But was it too late? Was the city tainted by association? Austin's penchant for unfettered free expression had allowed Jones to grow his platform, and its tolerance for his reactionary politics had come home to roost. In a way, Austin was always the perfect home for him—the capital of a state whose top politicians regularly threatened secession from the Union, even if only to score political points and reinforce its uniquely independent status. Jones was among those interviewed by the US House select committee investigating the January 6, 2021, attack on the Capitol in Washington, D.C., as he had played a major role in promoting the "Stop the Steal" conspiracy that held Trump had in fact won the presidential election and not Joe Biden.

My friend Dan Solomon, a journalist with *Texas Monthly*, spoke to various experts on conspiracy theories and disinformation, and they confirmed that the way in which Jones has an impact, whether on the mindset of Austinites or on the country at large, is that he popularizes a particular worldview. "In Jones's reality, anything bad that happens in the world is actually staged by the government to take away guns, or start a war, or round up all the patriots and put 'em in camps—or whatever conclusion gets people to keep watching the show," Dan writes. Love him or despise him, Jones is good at articulating these crazy beliefs, and because of the media coverage he gets, you can't avoid him. He is everywhere—particularly if you live in Austin. And Dan concludes that even if Jones disappears into bankrupt obscurity, it's too late. ". . . his brand of disinformation is a wildfire that he may have lit but no longer has any real control over." That's the problem. Alex Jones may have once been, as Richard Linklater said, "this hyper guy that we'd all kind of make fun of," but his brand has grown so big that his warped worldview has seeped into the public consciousness—whether or not you agree with it. Today, it's everywhere.

ONE AUSTINITE WHO APPEARED ON Jones's Infowars show several times (and who was also, incidentally, photographed meeting Trump during his first presidential campaign) was Andrew Wakefield, a fellow Brit who moved to America with his wife and four children. Three years before becoming an expat like me, Wakefield had published a study in the prestigious British medical journal *The Lancet* suggesting a link between autism and the common measles, mumps, and rubella (MMR) vaccine, and at a press conference he'd called for its suspension. After the paper was published, MMR vaccination rates dropped, *The Lancet* retracted the paper, and Wakefield was struck off by the UK's General Medical Council (GMC) after it found that his work was fraudulent and promoted a connection between the MMR vaccine and autism that didn't exist. Wakefield, the GMC concluded, behaved in a "dishonest and irresponsible" fashion and "showed callous disregard for any distress or pain the children might suffer." (After he'd been struck off by the GMC, Wakefield launched a publicity drive to promote his book, which he titled *Callous Disregard* as a not-very-cryptic "fuck you" to Britain's medical council.) Ultimately, the *BMJ* (formerly the *British Medical Journal*) published a series of articles revealing that Wakefield was guilty of a deliberate fraud, picking and choosing data that suited his case and falsifying facts.

A couple of years after moving to the States, Wakefield helped launch an autism charity called Thoughtful House Center for Children in Austin, where he assumed the role of executive director and head of its research program. From his new base in the Texas capital, Wakefield would undergo a metamorphosis, from which he'd emerge as the poster boy of the anti-vaccine movement in America. I met him at the inaugural American Rally for Personal Rights, a large gathering in Chicago's Grant Park for "vaccine choice," and watched as he bounded onstage to whooping and cheering from the adoring crowd. Countless studies since the *The Lancet* paper have shown the MMR vaccine does not cause autism, but despite this Wakefield is unrepentant. He told me that the medical establishment that shunned him and his work was denying an epidemic, likening it to the 1950s before tobacco was known to be harmful. He possessed an astonishing amount of self-belief. Austin may not be known as a hotbed for anti-vaxxers, yet Wakefield had found a welcome home there because it is a place where, if you've been ostracized elsewhere, you can reinvent yourself, even if it's as a peddler of pseudoscience.

IN FEBRUARY 2010, SHANNON AND I would listen to a breaking news report informing us that a single-engine plane had flown into the Internal Revenue Service building off Research Boulevard north of the city. Joseph Stack, a fifty-three-year-old software engineer from north Austin, had deliberately targeted the tax office on a weekday morning when two hundred employees were just starting their workday. Incredibly, only two people died—including Stack. He left a rambling manifesto against US tax laws and the IRS, saying "desperate times call for desperate measures." Stack had moved to Austin from California following the dot-com crash, fresh from an acrimonious divorce. "Bye to California, I'll try Austin for a while," he wrote. "So I moved, only to find out that this is a place with a highly inflated sense of self-importance and where damn little real engineering work is done. I've never experienced such a hard time finding work. The rates are 1/3 of what I was earning before the crash." He'd remarried in 2007, but at the time of his death he was being audited by the IRS for failure to report income. Stack wrote that he was forced to cannibalize his savings and retirement before coming to the attention of the IRS. "Sadly, though I spent my entire life trying to believe it wasn't so," he concluded, "but violence not only is the answer, it is the only answer."

When Stack flew his plane into the IRS building, I realized I'd perhaps misjudged Austin. It wasn't just music fanatics, peace-loving hippies, and pot-smoking students that I was sharing my hometown with. Austin no longer felt like a safe haven, a special city with a slow-beating heart and a warm embrace, protected from the excesses of an America that at one time seemed like a distant place. Now it felt like we were just as much at risk as anybody anywhere else. But at risk of what? I knew people who used to listen to Alex Jones, who thought he was onto something. And as his ever-nuttier beliefs became more amplified, I wondered whether they were following him down this path to an even crazier place.

Texas isn't unique in offering a home to antigovernment or extremist groups. Organizations that espouse beliefs or practices that malign an entire class of people are all over the United States. Texas has an outsized number of them because it's got the second-largest population of any state. But in 2022, Texas led the nation in disseminating white supremacist propaganda, and the extremist group Patriot Front, which is based there, was responsible for around 80 percent of all those propaganda incidents nationwide. That year hate groups repeatedly disseminated racist and anti-Semitic flyers in Black and Jewish neighborhoods around Austin. They hoisted banners over highways, defaced schools with swastikas, and recruited members at anti-LGBTQ+ events. A year later a report by the Anti-Defamation League said the presence of white supremacist and anti-LGBTQ+ groups in Texas continued apace and that over a handful of years it had seen "alarming levels of extremist ideology and activity" there, including an almost 90 percent rise in anti-Semitic incidents. Austin wasn't immune. I'd seen scores of gun rights protesters gather outside the capitol with AR-15s and AK-47s slung across their shoulders, wanting to see more lax legislation. And in the summer of 2023, dozens of Patriot Front members marched through the streets.

"Austin? That ain't Texas." I'd heard the refrain numerous times since moving to America. They were referring to the fact that Austin was liberal and the state of Texas had a reputation as a bastion of deep red conservatism. But a few months after moving to Texas, I had interviewed the leader of a militia—one of many civilian armies scattered throughout the United States who believe their individual rights are being trampled. And I discovered that extreme libertarians don't much like any government, regardless whether it comes in blue or red.

CHAPTER 5

THE GENTRIFIERS

I n March 2010, we bought our first house in Austin. We wanted to live no more than five miles from downtown and discovered a new subdivision under construction just off Highway 183, along the banks of the Colorado. The house we'd chosen was a 1,450-square-foot single-story with three bedrooms on a quarter-acre lot. The price was $165,000. Nationwide, the average price for a new home that year was $221,900. In Denver, by way of contrast, it was $259,084. Eventually the developer planned to build two hundred homes on the site. We were the sixth, and when we moved in, during that year's SXSW festival, the rest of the subdivision was still a building site with piles of sand and gravel, excavation debris, and a lot of pissed-off wildlife. Rattle-snakes basked on hot asphalt in the middle of the road; a vast herd of deer munched on overgrown wild grass each morning, silhouetted by the sun; bobcats cowered under bushes behind the property; and one afternoon I had a close encounter with a mountain lion that, to this day, none of my friends or neighbors believe. We were right on the eastern fringes of town, where the city met the countryside; beyond the river, farmland stretched for miles. And while it was evident the housing development we now called home had made an obvious impact on the environment, we were also part of the rapidly advancing gentrification of Austin.

In fact, in the decade up to us moving into our new home, while Austin's population had expanded by more than 20 percent, it had also become the only fast-growing city in America with a declining Black population and one of the most income-segregated metro areas in the entire country. Around the time Shannon and I bought our house, the average annual income for an Austin family was around $50,000. In east Austin, a historically Black neighborhood, it was less than $16,000. Across the city, where the unemployment rate hovered around 4 percent and 17 percent of folks wanting to buy a new house were denied a mortgage, over on the east side the unemployment rate was 12.5 percent and 24 percent of its residents were denied a mortgage. Economically, it was like two different cities.

After we moved in, we'd regularly watch that herd of deer scatter into the brush and woodland beyond our subdivision as a man on horseback rode up from the underpass below the freeway nearby and across the empty lots of wild grass, sand, and concrete. His name, I later found, was Malcolm Vincent, and his family had lived just across the highway for generations. Together with his wife, Kamesha Brooks, Malcolm ran Roll'n Da Dice Stables, where several east Austin residents rented stalls and boarded their horses. It was unusual to see someone other than a police officer on horseback within Austin's city limits (the two-steppers at the Continental Club, Broken Spoke, and White Horse saloon who wore Stetsons were almost certainly hipsters cosplaying as cowboys). Malcolm learned to ride from his uncle Horace, an army veteran who now taught kids how Black cowboys and cowgirls helped shape the history of the West. For generations, these east Austin horse riders had called this place home. But now Malcolm cut a somewhat tragic figure trotting across the construction site, on what used to be empty land where he'd roamed for years, taking his horse down to the banks of the Colorado, not a soul in sight. Now his way of life was under threat—from people like me.

It's easy to think gentrification is something that happened before you moved in, but the truth is someone probably thinks you're the problem. Actually, while people moving into neighborhoods and displacing families who'd lived there for generations are the most visible signs of gentrification, they're not the root of it. Racist housing policies have for decades denied Black people access to the same kind of housing as white folk, and experts say gentrification is simply the result of a system focused more on creating business opportunities than on the well-being of citizens. So how does this all happen in real time? Back in 1979, an urban studies professor at MIT, Phillip Clay, laid out what he called the distinct stages of gentrification: First off, after a few "pioneering" gentrifiers move into a neighborhood, another wave of gentrifiers follows. Second, corporations (real estate companies, chain retail stores, etc.) seeking to profit from those gentrifiers, become the main actors in the neighborhood, which leads to corporate control. According to P. E. Moskowitz, "the only entities powerful enough to change and hypergentrify an already gentrified landscape are corporations and their political allies." But there's another stage—a precursor to Clay's stages of gentrification: city governments offering tax breaks and favorable zoning to enable it in the first place. Without that, the condo developers wouldn't move in. Most people think gentrification is the hipster coffee shop on the corner serving nitro cold brew, but that's a sign, not a cause. At a fundamental level, government policies that prioritize wealth creation over community repurpose cities as places that generate wealth for the rich instead of places that serve the needs of the poor and middle class.

ON THE EAST SIDE OF Austin near the intersection of Twelfth and Chicon Streets, not far from where we bought our house, there's a little redbrick building. A sign above the door says

"Galloway Sandwich Shop," although "Sandwich Shop" is a bit of a misnomer. Monday through Saturday, for the last twenty-odd years, Stephen Galloway has made his grandmother's soul food recipes—meat loaf, chopped steak, and catfish, with generous sides of potatoes, rice, mac and cheese, and greens—for loyal customers. Today, Stephen's café is one of the few Black-owned businesses left in this little corner of Austin that is rich in African American history, and he knows it won't be long before he too is effectively forced out of the place he's lived his entire life. I wanted to chat with Stephen about the changes he's seen in Austin and what's happened to his community. The day I visited he was preparing food under the watchful eye of his mom, Laverne. A TV was turned up loud in the corner, and customers came and went.

Now in her nineties, Laverne first ran a café in the 1970s in Bastrop, not far from the family farm: two hundred acres of Texas where Stephen's brothers still have horses and cows today. His dad, Ray Dell, later worked as a barber—the shop is still there today, next door to the café. Stephen said back in the day his dad helped a lot of politicians wanting to turn out the Black vote. He used to sweep up at the shop but never thought he'd one day run the family business himself. The youngest of six siblings (he said he was a mistake and "came along late"), Stephen grew up in a three-bedroom house in east Austin. His grandmother was the disciplinarian, but she had a soft spot for him and she'd sit him on her lap and read him Bible stories. Stephen attended Sims Elementary until seventh grade. The school opened in 1956, two years after the Supreme Court ruled that racial segregation in public schools was unconstitutional. Despite this, few families chose to integrate, and Stephen remembers Sims as an all-Black school that served generations of African American Austinites.

Stephen recalls the east Austin of his childhood as a quiet place where everyone knew one another; he said you could walk outside your front door and hear the wind blow. "Right now, at this time of day, it would be full of people walking up and down the street—all day long, walking and talking—then all of a sudden it was like a ghost town. There used to be bars and restaurants. It's all gone. Now you just hear cars going up and down the street all day." Stephen reckoned things began to change dramatically around 2005. I asked what he noticed first. "More police," he said. "Suddenly I was getting stopped three times a month. That never happened before." Some of his siblings who worked as police officers for the Austin Police Department told him not to argue: "Don't give them a reason." "No confrontation." "Let them write you a ticket and they'll just move on." Sure enough, a comprehensive review of police racial profiling data released that year by the Texas Criminal Justice Coalition (now the Texas Center for Justice and Equity) showed that Black Austinites were more than three times as likely as white people to be searched and that Hispanic people were more than twice as likely. At a city hearing the same year on the quality of life for African Americans in Austin, twelve student panelists said police made young Black people feel unwelcome. One man studying to be a chef at the Texas Culinary Academy said he thought they were getting pushed out of the city, and more than half said because of it they didn't plan to stick around after graduating.

That quality-of-life report, presented in March 2005, came at a particularly fraught time for Austin. The previous month, Midtown Live, a nightclub popular with the Black community, was destroyed by a fire. Six police officers and four dispatchers were subsequently disciplined for celebrating its demise, exchanging messages like "burn baby burn" and "I got some extra gasoline if they need it." What the report found, perhaps unsurprisingly, was that African American residents experienced a strikingly different quality of life from non-Black residents. True, compared with the national picture, they had one of the country's lowest

unemployment rates, but compared with the rest of Austin, unemployment among Black people was more than double that of
white Austinites. Black-owned businesses accounted for just 2.5 percent of the total, and the report found that whereas the city once
had twenty music venues and clubs targeting a Black clientele,
when it was published that number had dwindled to two: the
Victory Grill and Sahara Lounge. Between 1990 and 2000, Austin's
Black population fell from 13 percent to 10 percent. Nelson Linder,
the president of the Austin branch of the NAACP, said the exodus
meant they were leaving not just their properties but previous
generations behind.

Stephen Galloway told me everything has changed. Rents
have skyrocketed. Some people stayed; most left, selling up and
choosing to buy cheaper homes in nearby towns like Round Rock,
Pflugerville, and Manor. "The police did their job," he said. Today,
some of his old customers come back every now and again to see
him. They tell him they're glad he's still there. I asked whether
he gets sad thinking about what's changed. "No," he said. "I know
things are never going to stay the same. It's kind of like when you
grow up and you wish you were still a kid—it's that kind of feeling."
A friend of Stephen's who owned a convenience store across the
street recently packed up and moved to Florida after his rent
went up to $4,000 a month. Today that convenience store is a
nondescript office. Stephen pays $1,200 a month to rent the space for
Galloway Sandwich Shop. A couple of years ago rent went up $800
in one month. He said he'll leave when the price gets too high. He
knows that day will come. "Then I'll retire to the country. Back to
the family farm," he told me. "Feel the wind, go outside, maybe
pick up a fishing pole." At the end of the 2019 school year, the
elementary school Stephen had gone to—Sims—closed its doors
permanently. In the fifteen years up until it shut, enrollment of
Black students in the district plunged 44 percent.

I MET UP WITH THE NAACP's Nelson Linder one morning at the trailer he was using as a temporary office while his office building, a stone's throw from Galloway Sandwich Shop, was being renovated. He sat at a cluttered desk surrounded by books and paperwork and an array of electric guitars propped up on stands on the floor. "You're in a cultural heritage district right now," he told me as we walked outside into the car park and began strolling up Twelfth Street. "It's been designated by the council. But they're not preserving the culture and they're not promoting the businesses, so it's just a designation." Lip service, in other words. African Americans had left Austin because of the cost of housing, followed by poor schools, he told me. They were the key reasons—and they were interconnected. The housing disappeared, gentrification began, and the schools fell apart.

Interestingly, what was left, aside from a few Black-owned businesses on the east side like the sandwich shop and the barber next door where Stephen's dad worked, were the churches. Black folk may have moved out to far-flung places like Buda, Pflugerville, Taylor, and Leander, but a lot of those families came back to Austin's east side on Sundays to go to church. Churches were always the connective tissue in their community, and Nelson told me while these congregations no longer live in Austin physically, they help them stay connected culturally. But no one knows how long this'll last. New churches are cropping up in the towns they've moved to; they're establishing new communities. "But the old churches are still here. For now," he said.

Nelson grew up in Macon, Georgia, and came to Austin as a student in 1980 to study at what was then Huston-Tillotson College (now University) after a spell in the US Army. He's worked in the insurance business for almost four decades and runs the NAACP chapter in his spare time. Nelson's seen a lot over the years he's lived in Austin. He says he's watched his community "die and move on and the culture get lost." He started noticing a change in the 1990s when property values began creeping up. The real turning point—the decisive moment that would determine Austin's future—came in 2005, he said, when State Representative Todd Baxter filed a bill that would prohibit Texas cities from enacting what's known as "inclusionary zoning." Inclusionary zoning would have essentially ensured any new development include a portion of units that were affordable, or make developers pay into a fund for affordable housing elsewhere. "Affordable" meant housing affordable to families earning 60 percent or less of the median family income—$42,660 a year for a family of four. Guess what? Egged on by the Home Builders Association of Greater Austin, the Texas legislature passed Baxter's bill, and the state became one of only a handful in America to outlaw inclusionary zoning. It didn't take long for developers to descend like flies and ramp up construction of high-end homes and condos, redeveloping neighborhoods that were once affordable. It was a free-for-all.

The Texas Low Income Housing Information Service (now Texas Housers) put it like this: the investor-developer lobby "wanted increased densities and greater building heights in exchange for providing as little affordable housing as possible in order to maximize their profits." In 2008, the Austin City Council voted to adopt an ordinance supported by that lobby, allowing developers to build higher and denser units in exchange for them making between 5 and 10 percent of those units meet a new definition of "affordability." The new definition? In 2008, affordable housing in Austin now meant a two-bedroom apartment could be rented for about $1,500 a month. Nelson said that meant any chance at Austin having a genuine, workable, effective affordable housing initiative had fizzled out. People he knew on the east side couldn't pay their taxes; some were evicted. "The problem is that the wages Black and brown people are earning are not increasing with the cost of living. The real struggle is from the folks who live here and who built this city who've been pushed aside. There are two different Austins."

IN 2005, *HISPANIC* MAGAZINE AWARDED Austin the distinction of being the number one city for Latinos to live for the second year in a row. It was its cover story, no less. Hispanic people accounted for 30 percent of Austin's population, and it noted that the city had a vibrant cultural scene, a low crime rate, and— back then, probably for the last time—reasonably priced houses, the average of which was $154,000. And yet its electoral system seemed weighted against Hispanic participation in local politics: just one in seven council members was Latino. The then head of the Greater Austin Hispanic Chamber of Commerce said the city was still living under an old "gentleman's agreement," which allotted one seat for a Hispanic person, one seat for a Black person.

What's more, a report prepared by a community group into the proposed redevelopment of one particular Hispanic community warned of issues around gentrification and affordability. The neighborhood it referred to was the Saltillo district, a community just east of I-35. Activists told the city board that would be awarding the development contract that it would lead to the displacement of Mexican-American residents and would essentially signal a free-for-all to other speculators. One of those activists, Paul Hernandez, said: "You're going to be destroying this community." Today, 18 percent of the apartments in the Saltillo Development, an eight-hundred-unit apartment block in the Saltillo district, are categorized as affordable. You qualify for affordable housing if your income level meets the US Department of Housing and Urban Development definition—$93,450 a year in 2023 for a four-person household. The Saltillo Development is on land owned by CapMetro, which runs Austin's trains and buses. But CapMetro's in the transit business, not the affordable housing business.

There is a profound lack of affordable housing in Austin, but it's difficult to quantify because the last study was done before the pandemic. It's a safe bet to assume there are thousands in line. There are also a lot of people buying second homes and apartments for wealth building and investment—and those properties are not being rented out to those needing affordable places to live. A study by the National Association of Realtors showed that over 40 percent of homes sold in Travis County in 2021 were bought by companies and corporations paying in cash. At the state level, for all the people eligible for affordable housing, around one-quarter actually get it.

And it's not just those earning below the median family income in Austin who struggle to find housing. Even if you make the median income for a family of four, which, in 2022, was $110,000, you probably couldn't afford to buy a house in Austin. You're stuck between a rock and a hard place—you're not rolling in money, and yet you don't qualify for affordable housing. If you're a first-time homebuyer, you're often competing with people offering over the asking price, in cash, sight unseen, plus they're waiving the inspection. In 2022, the average price of a home in Austin was $537,000, and the time each spent on the market was eighteen days. You could rent, but good luck finding somewhere suitable. What's more, Austin had seen the country's largest annual increase in the cost to rent a one-bedroom property—an astonishing 108 percent, more than double that of any other city.

BACK IN 1979, A NEIGHBORHOOD group calling itself the East Town Lake Citizens published a thin, hand-drawn black-and-white pamphlet that took the form of a comic strip. On the cover was a group of Mexican Americans sitting on the front stoop of a house, and their speech bubbles served as headlines pointing to what was inside the pamphlet. "What are you going to do when they run you out?" one man asks. "Will you still have a home this time next year?" asks another. Two women sitting on the top step ask, respectively: "Are the city's plans for east Austin what you want?" and "Will you be able to pay your rent?" A little boy sitting next to them says, "Do you know that the Rainey St. area is now being destroyed?"

The story of Rainey Street is Austin gentrification in microcosm. Today, the district is synonymous with bachelorette parties and day drinking, with once-beautiful historic homes built in the 1800s converted into bars, now barely recognizable behind lights and awnings and beer posters. While some of the original houses were destroyed in a devastating flood in the 1930s, those were replaced with bungalows, and the community that developed there was largely Hispanic. Its prime location just west of I-35 and walking distance to downtown meant Rainey Street soon became the site of a pitched battle between developers eyeing the area for housing, hotels, and entertainment and preservationists. By the mid-1980s the preservationists had won, but it was a short-lived victory. All that effort to see Rainey Street awarded historic district status meant nothing when the city rezoned it in the mid-2000s to allow development to continue.

Brigid Shea and her husband bought a house on Rainey in 1995—a tiny one-bed one-bath that was kind of falling apart at the seams. Shortly after moving in, Brigid, who'd worked as a journalist at NPR but had turned her attention to environmental advocacy when she moved to Austin in the late '80s, found out she was pregnant, and she and her husband spent what little money they had fixing the house up so it was livable. They knew they'd be able to stay there only a few years—their son would need a room of his own—but as a toddler he loved finding baby snakes and other creatures close to the banks of the lake, and the family liked to hike along the trail on weekends. The little house soon grew, albeit metaphorically, on Brigid and her husband. But the city was keen to rezone Rainey as commercial, and many of their neighbors were equally keen to sell their properties at a premium. One neighborhood leader, Bobby Velasquez, whose father founded Austin minicab company Roy's Taxi in 1931, told Brigid the alternative was to sit around and watch the area slowly gentrify. "We were the only ones who said keep it residential," Brigid recalled. "And we ultimately felt we couldn't argue against it—it made tremendous sense for those families."

Brigid and her family moved out of Rainey in 2001 and immediately felt homesick. Eight years later, entrepreneur Bridget Dunlap leased one of the old homes there and turned it into the district's first bar, Lustre Pearl, setting in motion a chain of events that would culminate in this old Latino neighborhood becoming the booming entertainment area it is today. Dunlap soon launched three more bars in the Rainey Street district. Her website refers to her as the "Rainey Street Queen"—a visionary who transformed "the once residential neighborhood into one of Austin's most sought-out entertainment and night-life districts." She was a "pioneer," her website said.

This idea of people thinking of themselves as "pioneers" transforming the "urban frontier" is the language of gentrification. "Urban pioneers, urban homesteaders, and urban cowboys became the new folk heroes of the urban frontier," the geographer Neil Smith wrote. "In the 1980s, the real estate magazines even talked about 'urban scouts' whose job it was to scout out the flanks of gentrifying neighborhoods, check the landscape for profitable reinvestment, and, at the same time, to report home about how friendly the natives were." When a new apartment building opened in Manhattan's Times Square in 1983, its owners took out a full-page ad in the *New York Times* that announced the "taming of the wild wild West."

Brigid Shea's house was eventually bought by a developer who built what she described as a "hideous exoskeleton" on top of it in order to expand the square footage. In 2014, somewhat ironically, the original Lustre Pearl was itself forced to close to make way for a condo development, but Bridget Dunlap opened a new spot kitty-corner to the old location on Rainey. Sad at the loss of the original building ("the one who started it all; the one who got people coming to Rainey Street") Dunlap bought the one-hundred-year-old building off the new owner and had it transported east of the I-35 freeway. Her brand had now expanded and on its Facebook page, Lustre Pearl East is described as "the daughter of Lustre Pearl, the first darling of the Rainey Street revolution."

In the summer of 2019, the final holdout on Rainey Street listed his family home—the one his grandparents had bought in the 1940s—for $2.6 million. Today, the handful of houses that remain on Rainey are decorated in bunting and plastic beer posters, cast in shadow on every side by high-rise apartments and hotel developments. It's a cluster of mega towers. The Van Zandt, a hotel that, when it opened in 2015, dominated the skyline in Rainey is now dwarfed by its competitors.

I think everyone in Austin should know the story of what happened to Rainey Street and how it happened. But that thin pamphlet with the little boy on the cover asking, "Do you know that the Rainey St. area is now being destroyed?" is tucked away on a dusty shelf somewhere in the bowels of the Austin History Center.

ONE MORNING I MET UP with Talib Abdullahi on the grounds of the state capitol. A mutual friend had told me about a Black history bike tour of Austin that Talib had started a couple of years ago. Back in the summer of 2020, Talib mentioned his idea on Instagram and thought maybe twenty or so of his friends might show up, but his post went viral, and instead four hundred people turned out to cycle around the city and learn something about its racial history. He's from Houston originally but came to Austin for college; he majored in American studies at UT and, since graduating, has worked for Tito's Handmade Vodka and YETI in their events departments. He ran the bike tours in his spare time.

We began at the Texas African American History Memorial on the capitol grounds—a huge plinth that depicts the history of Black people in Texas, from the explorer Estevanico in the 1500s, through slavery, to African American musicians and NASA astronauts. Talib pointed out a couple of figures carved into the bronze panel dressed in prison clothes and working with tools—the capitol, which was reconstructed in 1885 following a fire, he explained, was built partially by prison labor under the so-called convict leasing program. This was at a time when Black people were thrown in jail for vagrancy, drunkenness, or not having a job. Talib also noted that the memorial sits parallel to a very large Confederate statue, beyond which are two more Confederate statues. "There's one for African Americans and three for the Confederacy," he said. Talib was there when this memorial was finally unveiled to the public in 2016, but the occasion was marred slightly by a counterprotest of a dozen or so neo-Nazis standing nearby.

WE SADDLED UP AND RODE a mile or so west along Twelfth Street. Today, Clarksville is an upscale west Austin neighborhood of multimillion-dollar homes and the occasional bougie grocery store, but it was one of the first freedmen communities west of the Mississippi, settled by former slaves emancipated after the Civil War.

Black folks were forced out of Clarksville by Austin's 1928 city plan. In fact many pinpoint the year 1928 as ground zero for what's happened to communities of color in Austin. The engineering firm Koch and Fowler was hired to prepare a plan that would deal with the growing city's street layout, zoning code, and civic spaces. Its report would turn out to be one of the most controversial documents in Austin's history. The majority of what its authors suggested was benign, fairly sensible even. It included recommendations for parks and boulevards and open spaces, civic centers, railways, schools, and cemeteries. The authors wrote that "play grounds and recreation facilities are as much a necessity to the health and happiness of people as are its schools, sewer systems, water supply, pavements, and drainage." They were prescient too, warning that there was currently an "absence of any plan for expansion [of the city] in an orderly fashion," that "skyscrapers are threatening to be built on Congress Avenue, thereby shutting off the view of the capitol building from the south." They also noted that "the life and growth of the city depends upon the facility of the flow of traffic, and whenever any portion of the city becomes so congested . . . [it] will have reached its maximum value and it will begin to recede."

But then they saw fit to address what they called the "race segregation problem." This, they concluded, "cannot be solved legally under any zoning law known to us at present. Practically all attempts of such have been proven unconstitutional." After the Civil War, Austin was considered something of a refuge for freed slaves. By 1880 it was fairly integrated, geographically at least, and the Supreme Court had expressly forbidden zoning laws that resulted in segregation. Koch and Fowler's city plan sought to circumvent that law. "Negroes," the report went on, "are present in small numbers, in practically all sections of the city, excepting the area just east of East Avenue and south of the City Cemetery. This area seems to be all negro population." The report's authors recommended the area in question—just east of East Avenue, or what is today I-35—become the "negro district" and that facilities and conveniences should be provided there as an incentive to draw Black people to it. This would, they wrote, eliminate the necessity to duplicate white and black schools and parks. In other words, Black people would be "encouraged" to move east of I-35 and south of the cemetery. The rest of Austin—the bits with those beautiful parks, boulevards, and open spaces and civic centers and uninterrupted views of the capitol—were for white people. It took only a few years for Austin to become geographically segregated, per the report's suggestions.

The legacy of these two short paragraphs, in what was an eighty-seven-page report, would be felt for the next century. As Eric Tang, an African and African diaspora studies professor at UT, told me, the 1928 plan comports with a general understanding that he's always had about white supremacy: "Its most devastating effects are often kind of codified into documents that pass for being technocratic."

THE CITY FORCED MOST BLACK people out of Clarksville by denying the neighborhood public services, ensuring that sewer lines ended just outside its boundaries and refusing to pave the roads, put in sidewalks, install running water, or pick up the trash. In fact it began dumping rubbish from other parts of the city in Clarksville to encourage residents to move. A handful of families remained, though—the holdouts—and some of their descendants still own those same properties today.

In the late 1960s, construction began on the MoPac Expressway, the nearly always congested highway that slices the city north to south along its western flank. MoPac destroyed a third of the Clarksville neighborhood. As Talib and I cycled along Clarksville's sleepy, winding streets in the blazing sunshine, he mentioned that if the homes here were in his native Houston, most of them would cost around $200,000. Because they're in Clarksville, they're more like $1.5 million. Today, the neighborhood founded by African Americans experiencing freedom for the first time is unaffordable for most people.

What's happened to Clarksville has been in the cards for some time. A study of the community from the tail end of the 1970s showed the Black population of the neighborhood had dwindled by 23 percent between 1977 and 1979, the Mexican American population by 33 percent. Meanwhile, the number of "Anglo" residents had increased by 18 percent. Of the fourteen low-income households that left Clarksville in the same period, eleven were renters and ten were Black. "Low income households, especially renters, are succumbing to the pressures of housing deterioration," the report said. "The trend is toward continued displacement, especially among Blacks." Then its authors turned their attention to goals—suggestions for stopping what was happening. "Arrest the decline in the number and quality of low cost housing units," they wrote. "Minimize displacement of low and moderate income residents... Encourage resettlement of Clarksville by low and moderate income persons." They recommended implementing a "rental house repair program" and a "tools lending library," advocated for property tax relief for low-income homeowners. And they suggested constructing new low-cost homes in the area.

Take a walk through Clarksville today. Open up Zillow on your phone and look at the house prices. Then ask yourself if any of these recommendations—made in 1979—were ever heeded.

TALIB'S TOUR FINISHED A FEW blocks away at a statue on the UT campus: an African American woman stands, hands on hips, looking determinedly toward the intersection of Twenty-Fourth Street and Whitis Avenue. This was the politician Barbara Jordan, who'd been a major leader in the civil rights movement and the first Black woman elected to the Texas legislature. Later, she'd become one of the first Black women from the South elected to the US House of Representatives. Her scathing speech at Richard Nixon's impeachment trial has gone down in American political history, and she was responsible for expanding workers' compensation and expanding voting rights legislation.

Talib pointed toward a historic home across the road from the statue, an ornate redbrick Victorian mansion with castle-like turrets and a wraparound porch that was built for businessman George Littlefield, who donated huge sums to the University of Texas. "Littlefield was essentially the Elon Musk of his time," Talib told me. "One of the most wealthy people in Texas. But he was a Confederate army officer who believed the university should be branded as a South-centric institution." Somewhat ironically, the nickname for the UT campus that endures to this day—the Forty Acres—is also the exact amount of land that Union general William T. Sherman promised newly freed slaves would receive after the Civil War. "Forty acres and a mule" was one of the most significant pledges given to African Americans. Made in 1865, it was over-turned later the same year by President Andrew Johnson, a white supremacist. Littlefield, who was also a slave owner, was appointed regent of UT in 1911. He also paid for several monuments to the Confederacy to be installed on the UT campus. While those monu-ments have since been taken down, Littlefield's legacy remains: Littlefield Hall is an all-female freshman dorm, the Littlefield Patio Cafe satiates students on campus, and the Littlefield Fountain honors Texans who died in World War I. Talib thinks it's really symbolic that Barbara Jordan's statue now stands here looking across the road at Littlefield's house—a belated acknowledgment of the contributions to the city made by the very people Littlefield sought to ostracize.

In 2018, the Austin City Council approved a new land de-velopment code that would determine how land could be used throughout the city, including what could be built and where. It was known as CodeNEXT, and the main thrust of it was to allow more "density" in Austin, which translated to more high-rise condos. But the $8 million process served only to pit urbanists against preservationists. At one meeting back in 2018, an east Austin activist told a local forum it had been heartbreaking and that the changes Austin had seen had destroyed a lot of the social fabric for communities of color. Protesters gathered outside city hall. The NAACP's Nelson Linder said there was nothing good about CodeNEXT "except for folks with money" and that it would "destroy what's left of single-family dwellings."

At the tail end of 2019, a group of local property owners sued the city. One of them, Mary Ingle, said that on Duval Street, where she lived, the city wanted to raise the building height limit from thirty to ninety feet. "You wouldn't see the sun," she said. By the spring of 2022, CodeNEXT was dead. Three appeals court judges in Houston agreed with a lower court that the City of Austin ignored state law in its plan to overhaul zoning rules, making clear that if the city wanted to rezone properties, property owners within a certain distance of those proposed developments must be informed and given the right to protest. At the time of this writing, based on those court rulings, the City of Austin is still weighing its options with regard to a new land development code, and it doesn't think it'll meet its original timetable for its adoption. Meanwhile, the city gets bigger and its economy grows, and nobody in any position of power seems willing to challenge the developers and put a stop to the stampede.

On March 4, 2021, Austin's city council passed a resolution that it hoped would right the wrongs of the city's past, publicly acknowledging and apologizing for the role it played in the enslavement, segregation, and discrimination of Black Austinites. Item 67, which passed unanimously, aimed to create a sustainable economic model to address those historic policy decisions. It makes for pretty remarkable reading. The second paragraph acknowledges that since the city's founding it had depended on slaves and had yet to address "allowing Black residents equal opportunities to enjoy" nearly two hundred years of progress since that time. And it recognized what the 1928 city plan did to freedmen communities like Clarksville. It also acknowledged a 2017 study that ranked Austin in the top quarter of the nation's economically segregated areas.

In addition to the apology and recognition of the scars the city had created through its policies, the resolution also tasked the city manager with writing a report, in conjunction with the historically Black Huston-Tillotson University, outlining the economic harm caused through "economic, health, environmental, criminal injustice, and other racial disparities." In other words, to place a present-day value on what's owed to Black residents. And it outlined the creation of a "Black Embassy," which would provide resources and support to existing and future Black-owned businesses. That report is still apparently being written, and no budget has been agreed on. When they're weighing up the amount they're going to throw at the project, with any luck officials will consider the incentives they've given big tech over the years—Samsung, for example, could be in line for an $800-million-plus rebate over twenty years if it builds its chip factory in north Austin. I won't hold my breath.

Meanwhile, in the summer of 2023, the African American Cultural and Heritage Facility, which had closed for a few years because of the pandemic, reopened, and Visit Austin, the city's official visitors website, devoted a section to Six Square, encouraging tourists to explore Austin's "Black Cultural District"—the "six square miles of East Austin, originally created in 1928 as the Negro District by the Austin City Council," and "dotted with notable historic homes, churches, commercial buildings, schools, cemeteries, and parks."

The city adopted another resolution too. Known as the Right to Stay and Right to Return program, it would offer Black families or their descendants who had been displaced the chance to move back to the city by putting them ahead of the queue for affordable housing. Officials took inspiration from cities like Santa Monica, California, which in the 1950s and '60s had displaced a lot of Black families with so-called urban renewal projects—parks and freeways that required whole neighborhoods (read: Black neighborhoods) to be demolished. Recently, that city has taken steps to address the devastating effects of those policies.

In Austin, the first attempt at putting its money where its mouth is will be a north Austin development that will include hundreds of affordable homes for working-class families currently living in rapidly gentrifying neighborhoods, as well as those who have been displaced. Some, though, think it's just lip service; that instead, the city should be helping people like Stephen Galloway, who has run Galloway Sandwich Shop for more than twenty years, own his space, keeping that kind of cultural asset in the community. Instead, people like Stephen, living on the east side, are constantly harassed by flyers and people lowballing them with offers to buy their houses for cash.

The right to return is helpful, but so are better schools in Black neighborhoods and, as several Black Austinites told me, a new attitude that white liberals moving into historically Black neighborhoods could adopt—one where they'd get to know their neighbors rather than build high fences around their homes; one where they'd stop calling the cops on them; one where they'd ask, "How am I being a valued member of the community rather than making the current residents feel like they have to make me feel comfortable?"

YOU CAN'T REALLY GET INTO the weeds of gentrification in Austin without encountering Eric Tang. He's a professor in Black history based at UT and kind of the go-to guy on the subject in the Texas capital. I wanted to ask him what Austin's got right and what it's got wrong in addressing racial disparities that have plagued this city for so long. Usually local government officials go to people like Eric to ask them to prepare reports on subjects like this and offer solutions. In fact the City of Austin did just that a few years back when then mayor Steve Adler put together the fancy-sounding Task Force on Institutional Racism and Systemic Inequities. Eric was cochair of one of its subcommittees, and his subsequent report made several recommendations to redress racial inequalities in housing. So what happened after the report was published? I asked him this one morning over coffee at the Mueller development near where he lives. "It collected dust," he said, before taking another sip. "We produced some document, and here we are."

Eric thinks the key thing Austin could do is to have an actual affordable housing program; right now, he says, it has one in name only: "We don't have anything that resembles a kind of state-mediated or state-regulated affordable housing agenda or program." What Austin has instead is an agreement with developers that when they construct new housing they consent to sell a portion of those units to low-income residents. But there are two problems with this: One is that these low-rent or low-cost units don't have to be low-rent or -cost forever. Two is that there's no real regulation anyway, and that's what frustrates Eric most: "If I violate it, there's nothing that really happens to me."

In the summer of 2022, the city council passed policies allowing developers to build taller high-rise buildings—on the condition they provided more affordable housing. But there's a lot of skepticism. Eric thinks the city could put land it owns in trust and build housing on it in partnership with private developers. That way the housing could be affordable forever. Instead, he said, you've got a situation where deals are made with developers in return for them promising affordable housing, and it never quite happens the way everyone envisaged. Another issue, Eric told me, is deciding who actually qualifies for the housing once it's built. It's supposed to be people making less than the median family income, but it often isn't. "I love my grad students," he said, "but they make that median family income, or MFI. Let's go back to who really needs it. Take a look at what Denver has done, what Portland has done, and then look at Austin and draw your own conclusion. Denver has instituted a kind of 'development fee,' so if there's a developer who wants to build X number of square footage, for every X amount of square footage over this threshold they have to put money into a fund to pay for affordable housing elsewhere. In Texas, the state legislature—being the radical extremists that they are—passed a law prohibiting any municipality from doing this. And so City of Austin leaders were like, 'Hey, our hands are tied.'"

Eric doesn't know if there's a way around it, but he thinks Austin city officials threw in the towel too easily. And the exodus of born-and-bred Black Austinites continues apace—and with them, Eric said, goes a crucial political voice, and the sense of solidarity and mutual aid that African American communities established in order to survive the inequalities of Jim Crow, and a piece of the city's history.

CHAPTER 6

TOXICITY

In 2010, our friends Dwight and Jess bought a cute little house on a corner lot near Bolm Road and Airport Boulevard, a couple of miles away from us. Directly across the street from their house, behind a mix of aluminum and wood fencing, was a large swath of empty acreage—a mix of soil, old concrete with weeds sprouting from the cracks, and trees. When they were buying their place, Dwight and Jess tried to find out what it was, but nobody gave them much of an answer—their real estate agent never mentioned it, and one neighbor who had lived on the road her entire life told Jess it had once been a paper recycling center and that the neighborhood had fought to shut it down because wind would blow paper and debris into surrounding yards. Dwight and Jess didn't think much more about it. The vast fenced lot stood empty, but trees and bushes obscured it from the road.

It wasn't until after their twin girls were born in 2014 that they first heard about "toxic tanks" that once dominated this little corner of Austin: circular white silos towering above single-story ranch homes that were built on that plot. "When someone tried to develop the land, notices went out to neighbors about those tanks that had been there," Jess told me. "That was the first time we'd heard about it." The land, which had been a pecan grove in the 1940s, was where the notorious tank farm had stood, and Dwight and Jess had been living in spitting distance of it for several years, completely oblivious to what it was and the trouble it had caused.

In early 1992, almost two decades before Dwight and Jess moved next door, state and local authorities had launched an investigation into a sprawling facility at Springdale Road and Airport Boulevard that contained fuel terminals owned by various oil and gas companies. For more than forty years they'd stored and distributed most of the gasoline Austin needed to function as a city there, but people living nearby had started to complain of migraines, dizziness and nausea, stomach pains, lesions, respiratory problems, and skin rashes, which they blamed on noxious odors coming from the plant. Because of these fears of contamination, the tax values of more than six hundred homes surrounding the tank farm had been slashed in half. Tests showed there was groundwater contamination beneath some of those homes, and an investigation by the *Austin American-Statesman* newspaper found hundreds of people living there were plagued by illnesses—findings that it said were supported by an analysis of millions of Medicaid records. The six oil companies that operated the fuel terminals—Chevron, Exxon, Mobil, Citgo, Coastal States Crude Gathering Company, and Star Enterprise, an affiliate of Texaco—all denied a link between the health complaints and their operations at the tank farm.

By the summer of 1992, Austinites were up in arms. Four hundred people demonstrated outside the farm, carrying signs that read "Wake Up and Smell the Benzene" and "Move the Tanks, Not the People." Despite their insistence they had nothing to do with the ailments, by February 1993, all six of the companies operating at the gas terminal had agreed to relocate and clean up any residual pollution. By 2001, pollution from the deserted fifty-two-acre site had found its way under a park and creek that fed the Colorado River—"An underground swath of contamination beneath Govalle Park and Boggy Creek," according to reports. The oil companies suggested letting nature take its course, but experts estimated that would take around fifteen years.

I had no idea about any of this until recently. I hadn't even heard of the tank farm, let alone its toxic spew. Although we didn't live nearly as close as Dwight and Jess did, it's disturbing that huge scandals like this can so quickly get consigned to the dustbin of history. Dwight and Jess thought that the site had been cleaned up, but today, Jess says she thinks there was some denial and avoidance on her part. "We had little kids; we owned the house; we couldn't afford to move elsewhere in Austin. Of course I wondered if we should be worried about any health concerns. We had intentions of growing a vegetable garden, and in hindsight I'm glad we didn't. Would it have caused me to hesitate to buy there if I'd known beforehand? I definitely would have hesitated. I wonder today why nobody told me."

Back when neighbors were protesting the site, they weren't only concerned about the air pollution; they were anxious about the soil becoming contaminated too, about toxic chemicals seeping into the ground and making their way into the creek and into the neighborhoods surrounding the tank farm. There's a photograph in the archives of one of the grassroots organizations that advocated for the place to be shut down. In the black-and-white image, Betty Allen, a neighbor who lived directly behind the site, shows sores on her hands from gardening in her yard that she said were caused by soil contamination.

IT MAY COME AS NO surprise to learn that Austin's east side has the weakest zoning restrictions in the city. The 1928 city plan, which essentially forced Black people to move to an area east of what is now I-35, also proposed that in addition to commercial and industrial zoning, the east side should also embrace "unrestricted" building. The east side became a free-for-all. Today,

African American communities may be being displaced, but this wasn't before heavy industry had a chance to spew its toxic air all over their communities, with no concern for the long-term effects on their health. As a result of the Koch and Fowler plan, most industrial zoning in Austin was destined for the east side, and communities there have been fighting for decades to clean it up. I think it's important that people living in Austin today, particularly those moving into the city's "cool" east side, know its environmental history. Even if you don't think it impacts you directly today, it could tomorrow. Besides which, you owe it to the residents who lived there before, and who were disproportionately burdened by pollution and toxic waste, to understand the legacy of environmental racism in Austin and the resilience of the east side community that existed before you got there. Also, knowing about and understanding a city's past can inform its present and future, because perhaps we won't make the same mistakes again.

In 1962, the marine biologist Rachel Carson's book *Silent Spring* blew the lid off big industry's use of pesticides and its devastating impact on the environment. One section of the book chronicled how, shortly after sunrise on January 15, 1961, dead fish began appearing in Town Lake, stretching for five miles along the river east to Longhorn Dam. By the following day, reports came in that dead fish had appeared fifty miles downstream of Austin; a week after those first fish appeared, there were more a hundred miles away. Officials from the Texas Game and Fish Commission traced a noxious odor from storm sewers all the way back to a chemical plant on—guess where—Austin's east side. The company in question was Acock Laboratories on East Fifth Street that manufactured insecticide. Among the products Acock produced were DDT, benzene hexachloride, chlordane, and toxaphene. Its manager admitted that quantities of powdered insecticide had washed into the storm sewer and that disposal of insecticide spillage in that way "had been common for the past 10 years." The Game and Fish Commission predicted that even without further pollution, the river's fish population—which included catfish, bullheads, sunfish, bass, carp, mullet, eels, gar, and shad—would be altered for years to come. Some species, it said, might never recover. According to the *Austin American-Statesman*, a civil jury refused to pin blame exclusively on Acock for the fish kill, but the Game and Fish Commission would later cite and fine the company.

For decades, Austinites watched smoke billowing skyward from another controversial east side polluter: the Holly Street Power Plant, a sprawling complex of concrete and steel that since the 1960s had generated electricity from its location on the northeast shore of Town Lake. Over the years there had been fuel spills (in 1991, ten thousand gallons leaked from the plant) and fires, and those combined with noise pollution had led to a barrage of complaints from residents of the Holly neighborhood, a largely Hispanic enclave, who called it "environmental racism." The power plant was also just blocks away from a school. It finally closed in September 2007, by which time property developers had already begun to speculate.

Then there was the case of Pure Castings Company. Since 1968, the business had poured molten metal in the manufacture of industrial parts at its thirty-five-thousand-square-foot foundry on East Fourth Street. In 1992, officials from the Texas Air Control Board said Pure Castings was emitting an abnormally high amount of smoke into the air and successfully urged officials at the company to stop using the furnace until they fixed the problem, which was irritating teachers and students at nearby Zavala Elementary School. In 2008, neighborhood complaints about pollution from the facility escalated. The Texas Commission on Environmental Quality installed an air quality monitoring station and, while the air quality readings did not rise above accepted levels for air pollution, one former environmental chemist associated with the Eastside activist group People Organized in Defense of Earth and Her Resources expressed concern about fine particles that might elude detection. Such fine particles, he said, could penetrate deep into lung tissue—particularly worrisome close to an elementary school. Pure Castings relocated to Lockhart in 2016.

In total, Eco-Change Exchange, an alliance of community groups, estimates over 90 percent of Austin's industrial zoning was placed on the east side, and the community fought for years to clean it up. The east side of town is referred to as a "desired development zone." Meanwhile, over on the west side of town, since the 1980s, neighbors and community groups there have mobilized to thwart development and preserve the area. West Austin is still the "City Beautiful."

WEST AUSTIN IS A GATEWAY to the Texas Hill Country, the southernmost extension of the Great Plains—that vast area of mainly prairie that slopes eastward from the Rockies and down into Texas. Technically the Hill Country is the Edwards Plateau, a bedrock of limestone on which is a savanna that encompasses hills and cliffs, clear spring-fed streams and rivers, and an abundance of cedar, oak, mesquite, and brush. The Edwards Aquifer, which lies underneath the eastern edge of the plateau, is an underground labyrinth of porous rock that harbors the primary source of drinking water for two million Central Texans, not to mention water for agriculture, industry, and recreation in the area. There are a number of waterways that wind their way across the Edwards Plateau and help recharge the aquifer. One is Barton Creek, which rises near the town of Dripping Springs and flows for around forty-five miles from its source until it meets the Colorado River.

For decades now, demand for water by a growing population has stretched the aquifer beyond its capacity. You wouldn't know that in the height of summer, plunging into the springs from the diving board or swimming laps with goggles on, looking at the tiny minnows or mosquito fish darting beneath you, as we often did to escape the oppressive heat.

In 1949, then US senator Lyndon Johnson called for a comprehensive water program that would take into account the needs of Texas. "With its growing industrial and agricultural needs [Texas] faces some critical problems with respect to water," Johnson, who said his experience had been largely on the Lower Colorado River, wrote. "Our cities and industries are experiencing difficulty in obtaining adequate water supplies." More than sixty years later, those industrial and agricultural—and domestic—needs are greater than at any time in the state's existence, and Texas faces even more critical problems with respect to water.

For most Austinites, Barton Springs is the most visible sign that the city sits on an aquifer at all, and Austin's "natural swimming pool" essentially serves as the canary in the coal mine to assess the health of the water below ground. Since the mid-1990s, thousands of acres in the Barton Springs segment of the Edwards Aquifer have been subject to intense development, and Gregg Eckhardt, an environmental scientist who's been studying the aquifer since the early 1970s, fears for the future water quality of the springs, which sees thirty million gallons leak from its pores every day. Decades ago there were warnings it could be in jeopardy: in 1986, a report for the US Department of the Interior said urban development over the aquifer had led to concerns about the availability and quality of water actually in the aquifer. In 2003, Barton Springs closed for three months after high levels of arsenic and benzene were found in the pool—not enough, apparently, to pose a threat to human health, but attributable to the urbanization of the area, according to Eckhardt. A few years later the US Geological Survey said the springs contained low levels of the herbicide atrazine, chloroform, and the solvent tetrachloroethane, and in 2011, another report showed high nitrate concentrations, which it attributed to algae blooms ultimately caused by human waste. Over the years the fallout from developments along several miles of Barton Creek has included wastewater entering septic fields and leaching into the aquifer; rainfall that washes oils, hydrocarbons, and pollutants from the roads into the creek and springs; and fertilizers and pesticides that percolate from lawns and golfing greens into the waterways.

In 1990, a group of Austinites formed the Save Our Springs Alliance, a coalition of citizens concerned about a huge development proposed for the Barton Creek watershed. The Barton Creek planned unit development remains, according to the alliance, one of the largest planned developments ever proposed for the city. It called it a "monster." At the helm was Jim Bob Moffett of mining company Freeport-McMoRan and Robert Dedman, CEO of ClubCorp, the largest golf and country club operator in the United States. They sought city approval for a four-thousand-acre development that would include a million square feet of commercial development, 2,500 houses, 1,900 apartments, and three golf courses. The city council meeting that convened to hear the application on June 7, 1990, is by all accounts fairly legendary. Eight hundred residents stood up to speak throughout the night against its construction, and at 5:30 the following morning, the council unanimously voted to deny it. But it was far from over.

The denial of Moffett and Dedman's application sent, in the words of the alliance, "a shockwave throughout the development community, giving rise to lawsuits, threats of legislative action, and backroom dealmaking," not to mention plenty more city council meetings. A task force comprising developers and environmentalists reported back to the council that the level of mistrust between the two sides had become so intense that dialogue or cooperation was impossible. Perhaps it was because those opposed to development had roped actor Robert Redford into a high-profile fundraiser. Regardless, two years later voters overwhelmingly approved the Save Our Springs water quality initiative, an ordinance that dramatically limited what developers could do in the watershed, including further restricting the amount of impervious cover above the aquifer—buildings, sidewalks, and roads from which rainwater can run off into creeks rather than seep into the ground. The developers were furious, and the Austin Chamber of Commerce said the SOS initiative was legally and scientifically questionable, pushed by environmental extremists.

While newspaper editorials have waxed lyrical over the decades about how Barton Springs is the great leveler—how college students, bankers, lawyers, and mechanics benefit from its life-giving waters—others have noted the lack of racial diversity among its visitors. When the Save Our Springs debate was raging, one employee of the city's environmental division, while acknowledging it needed protecting, said Barton Springs was not really on the radar of a lot of people of color: "There are little Chicanitos from this side of town [east Austin] who have never even seen it. Barton Springs is not in their frame of reality." While all eyes were fixed on efforts to preserve a huge slab of underground limestone and limit any development in west Austin, some were (rightly) concerned that problems on the east side were mounting. That's not to say Austinites shouldn't continue to protect the springs— they're a barometer of the health of the city's water, after all. But for so long the emphasis on the springs and the aquifer and stymying development on the west side of town came at the expense of the east side. If Austinites can rise up and stop environmentally damaging development from happening on the west of town, they can do the same on the east.

IN THE FALL OF 2021, a few months after Dwight, Jess, and the kids sold up and left Austin for good, their southeast Austin neighbors learned that Austin-Bergstrom International Airport was about to build a multimillion-gallon site to store airline fuel (the airport claimed residents were told about the project several years before, but several said they were never notified). The airport was expanding in order to service the city's growing population, not to mention the huge rise in the number of visitors. The site for the fuel storage facility would be off Highway 183, between McCall Lane and Metropolis Drive, not far from where I used to live. As if history was repeating itself, some of those neighbors, concerned about fuel tanks leaking or catching fire and the implications for their health and on their property values, began a campaign to halt construction. One petition to be sent to the Austin mayor and the city council read: "History has shown us tank farms will lead to groundwater contamination, pollution, and cause high cancer rates and severe health issues for the community nearby." But their efforts largely fell on deaf ears. The airport's CEO, Jacqueline Yaft, wrote that there was no parallel between the east Austin tank farm and the proposed airport fuel storage site. Meanwhile, several tracts of the former tank farm site off Airport Boulevard could become housing under a proposal to re-zone. At the time of writing the Texas Commission on Environmental Quality hadn't confirmed the site was safe for residential use.

What happened on Austin's east side is a stark reminder that environmental racism is real and that the fallout from industry in residential areas can have a profound impact on the health and well-being of the people who call them home. But they're not just a relic of Austin's past. They can have a ripple effect—children who live in areas with high levels of air pollution are more likely to develop asthma and other respiratory problems. What's more, the industries doing the polluting are also major emitters of green-house gases. It's important to remember that climate change and ensuing extreme weather events such as floods, droughts, and wildfires, while affecting all of us, disproportionately impact marginalized communities. And as climate change worsens, these issues become more intractable.

CHAPTER 7

HOT IN THE CITY

We'd not been in our new house a year when, in the winter of 2010, Shannon found out she was pregnant with Olive. As we dug out our sweatshirts and jackets for the occasional frost that we knew Austin would see in January or February, we were oblivious to what would come our way as the new year dawned. The drought that lasted from 2010 to 2014 would see the hottest and driest 12-month periods on record, and by some measures it was even more severe than the 1950s drought of record, which lasted seven years and which set the goalposts for water planning into the future.

A few years before, drought had driven up the price of hay for farmers. Jacob's Well, an artesian spring and popular swimming hole in the Hill Country that usually released thousands of gallons of water a day, dried up for only the fourth time in its recorded history. The parks department responsible said it was due to a combination of drought and increased levels of groundwater pumping. By June 2008, the Edwards Aquifer Authority called for cutting water usage by 20 percent. Meanwhile, the cyclist Lance Armstrong, one of Austin's favorite sons who was still a few years away from being outed as the ringleader of the most sophisticated and successful doping program in the history of the sport, managed to come out on top of a particularly unfashionable list: the most egregious household water users in the city. In July of 2008, Armstrong used 330,000 gallons of water at his one-acre property—thirty-eight times the amount of water his neighbors used. His bill that month was $2,460. The *New York Times* called him the "Champion Guzzler of Austin Water."

In 2011, Texas saw a little under fifteen inches of rain, making it among the driest years in the state's history. After work each day, Shannon would walk through our subdivision down to the Colorado and submerge herself in the cold water, sitting on the silty riverbed with just her head above water, one hand holding a book. This was her only respite in a summer that would see ninety days over 100 degrees Fahrenheit, breaking a record set in 1925. Our daughter, Olive, was born at the end of July that year. Her first month on Earth, Austin's meteorologists announced, was the hottest in the city's history—a record that was finally surpassed in 2023. Downtown, a piece of guerrilla street art read: "Coming Soon! A Vast Desert." We brought Olive back home, where the air-conditioning was set to 72 degrees Fahrenheit. Even our dog, Scruff, had had enough. I could see that jumping in the river felt glorious, but walking the quarter mile back to the house made him wonder whether it had been worth it—the pavement was so scorching under his paws, I'd have to carry him most of the way.

One thing that did like the climate, however, was fire. For wildfires to happen, they need three things: oxygen, heat, and fuel. And thirty miles east of Austin, Bastrop, a pretty town down-river, had those things in abundance in the late summer of 2011. It's known as the Lost Pines region of Texas—a thirteen-mile belt of loblolly trees on the eastern edge of the town, mysteriously cut off from their sisters a hundred miles away in the Piney Woods, a forest that stretches from east Texas through Arkansas and Louisiana. That September, somewhere in the midst of those Bastrop pines, a tree crashed into overhead power lines, which in turn ignited the brush on the forest floor. The intense heat, combined with strong winds caused by nearby Tropical Storm

Lee, conspired to produce the perfect touch paper. The Bastrop County Complex fire would turn out to be the costliest and most destructive wildland fire in Texas history.

At our house in Austin, the smell of acrid smoke got more intense as the day wore on. Neighbors worried the fire might reach Austin; after all, that April, the Pinnacle fire had breached the city limits, destroying or damaging twenty-one homes. Earlier that summer I'd watched as firefighters extinguished patches of grass on the roadside just outside our subdivision. One cigarette tossed from a car window onto the verge was all it took. Shannon's uncle and aunt lived in a home in the heart of those Bastrop woods. Thankfully they were in Austin that day, but as police set up roadblocks on the eastern edge of the town, none of us knew if their house had survived. I volunteered to drive to Bastrop to find out, and as I approached the barricades still being set up across Highway 71, on the edge of the state park, smoke loomed on the horizon like a thick gray curtain hanging down over the forest. Thanks to Shannon's aunt and uncle thinning out some of the trees around their house and planting a type of drought-tolerant grass that harbors water, their home survived. A little guest house on the property wasn't so lucky, becoming one of 1,645 homes destroyed. Nearby Bastrop State Park was decimated. A couple of days later, all that was left were black spindles where there had been towering green pines.

A few years later, a report by the City of Austin would acknowledge what was plain for all to see: the impact on the city of this unprecedented heat, drought, and wildfire would lead to vegetation, tree, and ecosystem loss; diminished water supply; and poor air quality that would cause asthma and other breathing disorders. Wildfire, drought, extreme heat—these were no longer one-in-a-hundred-year events. These were becoming the norm, and anyone who, like us, had chosen to make Austin home had better get used to it.

Low water levels in Lakes Travis and Buchanan persuaded the Lower Colorado River Authority's board to approve an emergency plan to cut off water to rice farmers downriver, the result of which was that in some areas production dropped by at least 75 percent. That October, the *Statesman* published its annual list of egregious domestic water users. And once again, there was Lance Armstrong, alongside health care industry magnate Robert Girling, Republican US representative Michael McCaul, and prominent Texas lobbyist Neal "Buddy" Jones. Armstrong and McCaul had used between thirteen and twenty times the amount of water as the average Austinite. And this during one of the worst droughts in Texas history.

With droughts like this intensifying and becoming increasingly common, what's the impact on the city? Dowell Myers's quality-of-life study, when it was released in the mid-1980s, said locals often referred to Austin's laid-back lifestyle, which Myers said was a product of "summer heat" reinforced by "an abundance of water resources for recreation." Yet climate change is threatening to erode many of the factors that made Austin such a desirable place to live, and persistent droughts will have a devastating impact on the city's water supply, its natural environment, and its economy. Climate change is also exacerbating air pollution and heat waves, which are particularly dangerous for vulnerable populations such as the elderly and the homeless. And it's only going to get worse as climate change makes extreme weather events more common.

ONE MORNING I MET UP with my pal Forrest Wilder to take a kayak trip along Lady Bird Lake—the section of the Colorado River that flows through downtown Austin. In 1960, the river was dammed to create what used to be called Town Lake to provide a cooling pond for the Holly Street Power Plant. A Texan with a stuck-on ball cap and days' old stubble, Forrest's a keen outdoorsman. He's also a fellow journalist who specializes in environmental reporting. We launched our kayaks just south of the Tom Miller Dam and paddled around Red Bud Isle. Now a dog park, the island was created in the early 1900s from granite boulders left over from the catastrophic collapse of the dam designed to hold back the water in Lake Austin. As we paddle past it, the towering cottonwoods, live oaks, and cypress trees act as a sound buffer against the yapping of dogs.

It's hard to envisage what Austin looked like back then when you see the skyscrapers that dominate the city's skyline today, but eighteen feet below the hulls of our kayaks, its history is there in the mud and sediment: relics of a long-gone settlement that would one day become America's most talked-about city. A little farther upstream, in the Highland Lakes, archaeological digs in the 1930s uncovered rock shelters, burial grounds, knives, axes, skeletal remains, and other evidence of the hunter-gatherers who wandered these river valleys following bison herds ten thousand years ago and the early inhabitants of the banks of the Colorado. It's a safe bet to assume such artifacts would emerge from the silt and mud if you scoured underneath the concrete, rebar, and debris that litter the bed of Lady Bird Lake. If finds at nearby Lake Austin are anything to go by, the blue-green water of Austin's downtown lake also conceals bison bones dating back centuries, earth ovens and spears once used by our early ancestors, and bottles, tin cans, brooches, muskets, and cookware owned by the pioneers who settled here later on. They are the men and woman who paved the way for the Austinites of today. But neither those hunter-gatherers nor those early settlers could have imagined the sheer number of people whose lives would depend on the water source they had taken for granted or that in the future a warming climate would stem its flow even more.

Actually, Forrest is surprised how little attention modern-day Austinites pay to climate. "Most of them spend their days inside their air-conditioned homes, so it doesn't affect them that much. A lot of them have no idea where their electricity comes from, where their water supply comes from. But," he told me, "I think there's a threshold in terms of climate change. And in the case of Texas there'll reach a point when people go: 'Oh, shit.'" Forrest also thinks there'll come a time when Austin's economy will take a nosedive, when the quality of life in the city will be so severely affected by climate change that people will leave or choose not to move there in the first place. "If I'm a twenty-five-year-old tech worker and I have a choice between a place that's unbearably hot for six months of the year versus one that's not, I know which one I'd choose," he said.

Forrest went on to tell me that, after the 2011 drought, he and his partner seriously considered leaving Austin. If that drought had happened again or become a regular occurrence, perhaps Shannon and I would have left sooner. His points were important ones. To stay in an increasingly hot climate meant utilities reaching an all-time high—another knock against affordability—and less chance you'll actually want to spend time outside, one of the reasons I'd first come to love Austin. It felt clear that the city, a place known for its heat, was an early indicator of the terrifying repercussions of global warming; whether we wanted to acknowledge it at the time, the drought was one of the first signs this climate would be pushed to new extremes.

An estimated half a billion trees in Central Texas were destroyed as a result of the drought in 2011. It took years for some of them to die. They became weak, then they endured other stiflingly hot summers and some freak cold snaps. Austin actually gets a fair amount of rain, but most of it comes in two flushes—in the spring and fall. Each time we'd get a monsoon-style rainstorm, we'd sit on our front steps with Olive and Scruff and marvel at the biblical amount of water falling from the sky. There's a wonderful black-and-white image captured by Harvey Belgin, a photographer for the now-defunct *San Antonio Light* newspaper, of an elderly man beaming with joy as he stands, hands raised above his shoulders, his shirt soaked in a rainstorm. This is the face of farmer Sam Smith—and Belgin snapped the picture in 1951 just as rain fell for the first time in months, soaking Smith's drought-plagued fields.

It's such a powerful photo, and in Austin, in summer, I thought of it often; I thought of it again after my conversation with Forrest, when we'd chatted about global warming's impact on Austin. Not that the drought itself was the only issue. The problem is the city seems to be in constant drought, even though it sees a lot of rain, because it's so damn hot and that exacerbates the rate of evaporation. There's so much water loss from evaporation that it stresses trees, plants, and grasses too much, and that's why we saw huge die-offs. One climate scientist told me that up in the Rocky Mountains of Colorado, tourists stop along the roadside to look at the beautiful red trees, but what they're actually looking at is a forest of dead trees. And it's happened because they're facing both drought and heat, which make them susceptible to native pests like the bark beetle that they'd normally be able to cope with. Losing trees in a city like Austin that is seeing hotter and hotter weather should be alarming to anyone, because trees are essentially nature's air-conditioning. Studies show that the air temperature directly underneath their leafy canopy can be as much as 25 degrees Fahrenheit cooler than that above nearby blacktop.

"Have you ever been to the spring over here?" Forrest asked as he began paddling toward the bank. "It used to be kind of a secret, but it's really not a secret anymore." I hadn't, so I followed him over to the southern edge of the river, just upstream of the MoPac Expressway. This stretch of Lady Bird Lake is quiet; the multimillion-dollar houses on the bluff above are too high to see from a kayak seat in the shadow of the limestone cliffs, and the south shore of the lake is devoid of much of anything other than trees. We pulled the kayaks up on some rocks, climbed out, and stood in the shallows. The water was clear, and you could see the sandy bottom and small fish darting in and out of the rock pools. Then, near the base of the cliff, a few inches above the waterline, Forrest pointed to where Deep Eddy Spring discharges cold, clear water from deep within the Edwards Aquifer into the lake. Twenty feet away there's another one, known as Cold Spring, doing exactly the same thing—the result of what's known as "artesian pressure" that forces water up from below the ground. I'd swum in Barton Springs countless times, but for the first time in twenty years of visiting or living in Austin I could actually see the reason for the city's existence, the reason those Native American tribes set up camp here ten thousand years ago, and the reason a pioneer called Jacob Harrell moved with his family to the edge of Shoal Creek back in 1835. The way Austin is able to sustain its population was literally pouring out of the earth.

A little farther upstream, I'd seen metal pipes crawling up the rock face like arteries, disappearing into the vines and trees above—conduits enabling those who lived in those multimillion-dollar homes to pump water, endlessly, from Lady Bird Lake up to their thirsty lawns, plants, and vegetable gardens in the sky. Forrest told me it's perfectly legal too. They were probably grandfathered in years ago.

There's only so much water in the aquifer. If we pump too much out of it, it stops flowing. In the 1950s, the Comal Springs system, the largest in Texas and also sourced in the Edwards Aquifer, stopped flowing. It dried up only temporarily, but climate scientists fear it's just a matter of time before it happens again. "No rain equals no water," Forrest said as he climbed back into his kayak and began to paddle slowly away from the springs. "And looking at the drought monitor last week, it's not looking good out there."

Farther downstream, past the MoPac and Lamar Boulevard bridges, Shoal Creek empties into Lady Bird Lake. I struggled to remember the view from this stretch of water before it was interrupted by the central library, the "Jenga" tower, and the rampant construction in the Seaholm District. In 1839, the year Austin was chosen as the infant Texas capital, the mouth of this creek roughly marked the far western limits of the city and was a popular swimming and fishing spot for the early settlers. Shoal Creek was a major crossing for bison, for Native American tribes hunting those animals, and for early Anglo and Mexican settlers before heading northwest into the hills.

Even farther downriver, past the Tom Miller Dam, where Lady Bird Lake ends and the Colorado River once again resumes its course, the opposite is true: here it's easy to forget you're in the city at all, and this is one of the few places in Austin today that probably looks similar to how it did before the city was settled. When Shannon was pregnant and submerged herself each afternoon in the river to keep cool, that stretch of the free-flowing Colorado felt—and still feels—remote. You're enveloped on both sides by pecan, cottonwood, mulberry, cypress, and sycamore, below which is a dense understory of dogwood, greenbrier, trumpet vine, buffalo gourds, and wild garlic. You hear the croak of cormorants, the occasional splash of a bass leaping from the water or a turtle plunging from a branch where it's been basking; you see egrets and herons stake out the banks and watch as swallows and hawks soar and swoop above the water. Beneath you are turtles and gar—the ancestors of which have been discovered in 215-million-year-old deposits of Permian-period sandstone and shale. In some ways this stretch of river is the barometer of Austin's water. When there's a severe drought, the Longhorn Dam will stop releasing water downriver, and this section will dry up first.

A STUDY IN 2020 FOUND climate projections for the twenty-first century showed "unprecedented" drought risk for the US

Southwest and Great Plains that would present "unprecedented challenges." Texas, it noted, was one of the fastest-growing states in the country, and while its water usage had historically been predominantly for agriculture, its population explosion meant the priority for water had shifted from rural to urban areas. As a result, it said, Texas was "water stressed" and that there was substantial uncertainty in the future availability of water in the state. The study's lead author was John Nielsen-Gammon, a meteorologist and climatologist at Texas A&M University and the state climatologist. He found that climate models that projected decreasing reservoir supplies in the twenty-first century were accurate, and Texas could expect drier conditions in the latter half of the twenty-first century than even the most arid centuries of the last one thousand years, including those that saw "megadroughts."

Nielsen-Gammon and his coresearchers wrote that Texas's water management strategy, produced by the Texas Water Development Board every five years to address the state's water needs over the next fifty years, was based on what they called a "rear-view mirror approach" that focused on historical data and drought patterns that, while effective, ignored a declining water supply related to future climate change. That water plan has already fallen short. Its goal was to have an adequate-enough water supply to meet the needs of Texas water users if the worst drought in the state's history ever returned. That drought, known as the "drought of record," occurred between 1950 and 1957, and it's already been surpassed. There will, the researchers concluded, be less water in reservoirs, and without new ways of storing water, Texas will no longer be able to support human activity. In short: those in charge should have started preparing for this apocalyptic scenario yesterday. The lack of preparation means that Austin is increasingly susceptible to fires and drought—and the impact of global warming will continue to have a visible and outsized effect on what used to be the "ideal residential city."

That's what Austin was called in the 1928 city plan, but that's probably because in the early 1900s, it saw heavy rains (and so much flooding that its dam collapsed). And now water is a precious commodity—in part because of who holds the rights to it. Texas courts have consistently ruled that landowners have a right to pump unlimited amounts of water from beneath their land regardless of the depletion of wells of adjacent owners, under what's known as the "rule of capture." Once that water comes out of the ground naturally, though—whether as springs, streams, or rivers—it belongs to the state. And now it's become an issue of the people.

ONE MORNING I MET UP with Sharlene Leurig for a drink on South Congress. Sharlene's the CEO of Texas Water Trade, a non-profit that looks to big tech for answers to how to ensure a future of clean, flowing water for the state. In Austin we use the words "aquifer" and "river" as if they're two independent water sources, but Sharlene said that doesn't mean much to the aquifer or river system in Austin, as it's the same water that flows back and forth between the two. And if we're pumping it out of one, it's going to affect water availability elsewhere.

"In Austin," she said, "the long story short is that if we do nothing about it, given population growth, given climate change, the Highland Lakes will go completely dry at least four times over the next hundred years." Ironically, one of the key attractions of Austin—its lakes, springs, and rivers, which persuade people to move here in the thousands—is being destroyed through this incessant demand for water. Sharlene described the situation to me, somewhat diplomatically, as insanely challenging. "If the lake drops below a certain level it's called a 'dead pool,'" she explained.

"And basically at that point you can't really pull any water out. Imagine you're in a multiyear severe drought and Austin's lakes become unreliable. What do you do?" Mining an aquifer for its water is fine for the first decade, two decades, even more, but ultimately, as a population increases exponentially, it'll run dry.

A task force established to determine what Austin should do if and when its water supply tanks looked to Australia to see what was happening there. Since the time of the Romans, Sharlene told me, we've been taking clean water and moving it to where a population needs it, and water pipelines, she said, are essentially an "aqueduct 5.0," but if we want to build something sustainable and local, there's no single solution that's going to serve a city like Austin for a hundred years or more into the future. Not to mention the fact that in 2020, Austin's water utility pipes leaked more water—7.34 billion gallons—than in any of the prior twelve years. That's enough to fill up Lady Bird Lake more than three times over.

Because of Texas's rule of capture, landowners in Austin whose property is on top of the aquifer can draw as much water from it as they want without consideration of the needs of other water users. Some cities have come up with innovative ways of tackling the problem this causes. In 2013, in Wichita Falls, north Texas, authorities there fast-tracked an emergency system to recycle its water after the devastating drought of 2011. The city of one hundred thousand draws its water from lakes that depend on rainfall that usually averages more than twenty-eight inches a year. In 2011, Wichita Falls saw only thirteen inches, and it wasn't much better the year after that. With the lakes severely depleted, the city set up its direct potable reuse (DPR) system, which blended treated wastewater with lake water before sending it back through the water treatment plant again. "It went right back into the city's drinking water supply," Sharlene told me. "And they did it because they didn't have a choice." In 2015, when the yearly rainfall returned to normal, Wichita Falls switched the emergency filtration system off. But it's ready should the city ever need to activate it again. The problem that keeps arising, of course, is that water's not an infinite resource. Once developers and cities realize that, they'll come up with innovative solutions. But what happens if they're too late?

The City of Austin came up with an idea to store huge amounts of water underground in existing aquifers. In other words, instead of hoping those vast underground water collectors will recharge naturally, utilities would pump water underground in times of flooding and store it for use in times of drought. The technique is known as "aquifer storage and recovery" (ASR), and by 2040, Austin hopes to store two and a half times the amount of water currently in Lake Austin underground, where it won't evaporate. In fact, there are two successful ASR locations in Texas already. One of them is in San Antonio, where the water authority takes excess water from the Edwards Aquifer when water levels are high and pumps it into the Carrizo-Wilcox Aquifer south of the city. In 2020, the Austin City Council approved a $6 million contract with an engineering firm to identify which aquifers could be good candidates for aquifer storage (including the Carrizo-Wilcox Aquifer).

The problem is the Austin project is at least two decades in the future, and twenty years is a long time when you consider how quickly the climate is changing. According to the Texas Water Development Board, the state will need an extra 10 trillion liters of water a year by 2070, and the big question is where and how it'll find it in time. There are also environmental concerns with aquifer storage. Opponents say it could lead to decreased stream and spring flows and a serious risk of contamination by arsenic, hydrogen sulfide, or uranium from fertilizers and pesticides—not to mention how energy intensive ASR is. It just all feels too after the fact. We've known for decades and decades that Austin's water was vulnerable, and not tackling it earlier is an unforgivable sin.

IN FEBRUARY 2021, A PREDICTED cold front caused the unfortunately named Electric Reliability Council of Texas, which runs the state's electricity grid, to urge residents to turn the heat down slightly and "unplug the fancy new appliances you bought during the pandemic and only used once." But ERCOT's advice proved woefully inadequate. Electrical outages began on the morning of Valentine's Day, when temperatures plunged into the single digits, with more than one hundred thousand homes and businesses losing power across the state. By the following day that figure had topped 4.5 million. Water pipes froze or burst. A friend in Austin posted a photo of a vast mass of icicles reaching from her outdoor faucet to the ground—like a lot of Texans, she wasn't aware that you don't drip the outside faucet to stop it from freezing. Austin just wasn't used to weather like this. As deadly Winter Storm Uri barreled through Texas, it left two hundred dead and millions without power. Residents were left without drinking water and food. The state's power grid all but failed completely.

Texas produces more wind power, natural gas, and oil than any other US state, but it's an energy powerhouse that also consumes more than any other state. The place responsible for giving us J. R. Ewing is oil country—and proud of it. But when the cold snap caused power plants to shut down and natural gas wellheads to freeze, it resulted in possibly the worst energy infrastructure failure in the state's history, and it was all caused by the deliberate actions of power generators, who resorted to rolling blackouts when demand overwhelmed supply. Those who weren't skiing down RR-2222 were huddled inside under as many blankets as they could find. Electricity prices for Texas households in some parts of the state hit nine dollars per kilowatt-hour, when Texans were used to paying an average of twelve cents.

What was most egregious was that it all could have been avoided. Ten years earlier a winter freeze caused another power crisis in Texas, but reports that cautioned such events could be far worse in the future went unheeded. The ice hadn't melted when Austinites began to ask who was to blame. Governor Greg Abbott said the fault lay with solar farms and wind turbines freezing. Sid Miller, Texas's agriculture commissioner, posted on Facebook that "we should never build another wind turbine in Texas." But Abbott and Miller, echoing the climate change denialism of their political party and attacking green energy, were wrong—or being deliberately deceitful. Natural gas, coal, solar, and nuclear plants all struggled, but the biggest failure of all came from nonrenewable energy sources: conventional gas-driven power plants.

Furthermore, Texas is the only state in the Lower 48 that is almost entirely disconnected from the power grid that the rest of the United States is connected to. This allows it to avoid regulation by the federal government, but it also means at a time of crisis it can't draw emergency power from neighboring states. In 1999, caving to pressure from the industry, then governor George W. Bush signed a law deregulating the state's energy market. This was designed to cut the industry's overhead and purportedly bring down the cost of electricity for all Texans by encouraging competition in wholesale electricity prices. But just a decade afterward, prices were higher than at the start of deregulation, and Texans were getting hit with bigger price increases—$28 million more for power than they would under traditional rates. A report published in 2009 said ERCOT had made expensive missteps since the beginning. Some of its executives had been subject to criminal charges and it was years behind schedule on a major market overhaul. A major problem, it said, was moving power from parts of the state where it was abundant to areas where it was needed most.

There was no reason Texas power plants couldn't have been protected from weather of the type Winter Storm Uri brought in February 2021. We have power plants *in the Arctic*. It just costs money. Letting homes and businesses choose their electricity provider sounds like a good thing. But deregulation also means less oversight, and Texas has the largest deregulated electric sector in the United States. Former Texas governor Rick Perry, who would later serve as US secretary of energy under President Trump, wrote in a blog post that Texans preferred rolling blackouts to more government oversight of their energy market. Ask those Austinites who lived under piles of blankets for days if they agree. After the storm ERCOT's CEO was fired and the head of the Texas Public Utility Commission resigned. The Texas legislature ordered regulators to ensure power plants were better prepared for extreme weather in the future, but after 210 people had died, it was too little, too late. The total economic impact to Texas was estimated at $195 billion on the low end and as much as $295 billion on the high end. Some described it as the most expensive natural disaster in US history. But it didn't need to be, because it was a winter storm that was entirely predictable.

Perhaps unsurprisingly, it was poor communities of color in Austin that were hardest hit by the storm, because they tended to live in neighborhoods with older homes with bad insulation, older pipes, and roofs prone to leaking. They suffered cracked pipes, collapsing ceilings, electrical issues, and even pest infestations because of exposed walls and damaged drywall. Some Austin residents reported mushrooms growing out of their carpets and mold on the walls.

If Winter Storm Uri graphically exposed the deadly division between rich and poor in Austin, then what happened to the city's housing market afterward drove the nail even further into the proverbial coffin. Two months after the storm cast its icy pall, Austin's housing market would experience its highest increase in average home prices in the United States, beating out cities in California and Florida—a rise of almost 29 percent from the previous year.

I ASKED PETER BECK, A climate scientist at St. Edward's University, why he chooses to live in Austin, considering the seemingly intractable problem with its climate. He laughed. "I mean, right now it's not a theoretical question," he said as we sat in the shade of academic buildings in a little courtyard on campus in south Austin. "This is the hot place to be, and people just aren't thinking about ten, twenty years from now. But yeah, I mean, I wouldn't retire here." Beck said the climate is going to be a huge problem, particularly with Austin promoting endless growth and with all the people moving here. "We don't have tornadoes, we don't have earthquakes; we get some flooding events, but it's not like a coastal city where there are huge threats, you know. We're actually pretty good except for the heat," he said.

Heat is the major climate change issue affecting Austin and Texas, he told me, and in the near term, the easiest, cheapest, most effective way of tackling it is to focus on conservation: "Getting people to use less water; getting rid of their lawns." But also, Beck added, "the city could just stop encouraging growth." Meanwhile, in the coming years the drought west of the 100th Meridian is predicted to worsen. Today around half of the American West is in "severe drought," according to the US Drought Monitor, and climate researchers don't predict enough rain during rainy seasons to offset it. Austin's only going to get hotter. And drier.

CHAPTER 8

GHOSTS

One morning in 2010, we found a small business card inserted in the doorjamb that read: "House cleaning services—call Magali," with a local phone number. A week or so later, Magali (not her real name—she wanted me to protect her identity for reasons that will become apparent), a Guatemalan woman in her early thirties, was cleaning houses for us and several of our neighbors. After she'd been working for us for a year, Magali gave birth to her son—a few months, in fact, before Shannon had Olive. As the years wore on, he'd occasionally accompany her to our house, and he and Olive would sit on the couch in the living room watching cartoons.

During the years she cleaned for us we never asked her story, but I knew there was a story to tell. Magali was undocumented—we knew that much—and was married to a Guatemalan man who was also undocumented. Once, when we invited her around for a barbecue, she told us she and her husband were worried about driving at night; they feared something would happen to them if they were pulled over by the police. Some friends of theirs had been picked up by Immigration and Customs Enforcement (ICE) agents in the past, she said, and others had been deported. Although their son was a US citizen, Magali and her husband were forced to live in the shadows. I wanted to hear her story because I knew that it was the story of so many undocumented immigrants in Austin who were part of the glue that held the city together. They were Austinites like anyone else who called it home, and yet they felt like ghosts.

Magali told me she was born in Villa Hermosa, a small community of five hundred people in Guatemala, but she moved to the capital, Guatemala City, to study social work at university. During college she'd tried unsuccessfully to find a job; there was little economic opportunity, and the country was prone to natural disasters like earthquakes, volcanoes, tsunamis, floods, droughts, and hurricanes. The civil war between the government and leftist rebels, fought from 1960 to 1996, had resulted in political instability and saw thousands of Guatemalans flee as refugees to Mexico, the United States, and Canada.

Lack of economic opportunity is the single largest driver of "irregular migration" from Guatemala—that's the movement of people outside the international norms that usually govern entry or exit from a state. In 2005, an estimated 320,000 undocumented immigrants from Guatemala lived in the United States, and between 6,000 and 12,000 new Guatemalan migrants were crossing the US-Mexico border each year. Recently there's been an increase in the number of Guatemalan women crossing in order to provide for their families back home.

Magali made the decision to enter the United States in 2004, a year after I first arrived. She figured she'd go for a couple of years, save up some money, then return to Guatemala to carry on her studies. Making the decision to enter the United States sounds easy, like one day she woke up and just decided that's what she wanted to do and then traveled there. It was far from that simple.

Magali's two brothers and sister didn't want her to go; they said the family could live together in Guatemala City and she could carry on studying in a few years, once she'd found a job and saved some money. "They knew a lot of people who had died in the Río Bravo," she told me. "But I wanted to go." The Rio Grande forms the border between Texas and Mexico and is known as Río

Bravo del Norte—or just Río Bravo—in Central America. A friend
of Magali's who had successfully crossed and had settled in Austin
a few years before encouraged her to make the journey; she said
that for her it had been easy and that they could live together once
she'd made it to Texas.

In the early 2000s, Austin had a far lower cost of living compared
with that of major cities like New York, Los Angeles, and San
Francisco. It had a reputation—real or imagined—as a vibrant and
culturally diverse place with a strong sense of community that
appealed to many immigrants who may have had friends or family
there. There was the promise of work, and it had a thriving entrepreneurial atmosphere that encouraged small business start-ups.
Plus Texas shared a border with Mexico.

Magali's father didn't want her to go either but told her if it
was her dream he wouldn't stop her. A friend of hers also wanted
to cross the border into the United States, and she told Magali she
knew some people-traffickers who could take them and would
keep them safe. It would cost 16,000 quetzales, the equivalent of
$2,000. Magali's father offered to take out a bank loan against his
house to pay for the trip, and once Magali got to America and found
work she could repay him. "When my brother found out what my
father wanted to do he said no," she told me. "If I didn't make it to
the USA, who would pay the money back in order to take the title
back from the bank? My father would be evicted. The same thing
happened to some people we knew; they died on the border, and
their family lost their house, lost everything." But Magali knew
she wouldn't find a job in Guatemala. In the end, a family friend
loaned her the money. Her father insisted on accompanying her
to meet the people who'd be transporting her so he would know
where they lived. "In the end he never found out, though," she said,
"because we met them in a park in Guatemala City."

Two weeks later, Magali and her friend went back to the same
park to meet the men who would be taking them. It was July 2004,

a Sunday, around midday. There were twenty-three migrants in the park, each paying the traffickers, and a bus parked nearby, waiting to transport them. The first leg of the journey, to La Mesilla on the border of Mexico, took about two and a half hours. They stayed the night in a hotel, then the next morning the guides told them they needed to get away from the Mexican checkpoint. "We walked four hours into the mountains and across into Chiapas," Magali recalled. "It was very humid. We arrived at a farm, but there was another group there from Honduras and they were sleeping in the house, so we had to sleep on the porch. We stayed there for a week, and someone brought us frijoles, rice, and tortillas three times a day."

Magali figured they would be taking the same bus to the Texas border, but a week after they arrived in Chiapas a man came to the house with a truck that transported bananas, and it had a secret compartment where the migrants were told they would have to hide for the remainder of the journey. "My friend who came with me is tall, and she had to sit with her head to one side because she couldn't sit up straight," Magali said. "There were the twenty-three of us from Guatemala and about forty from Honduras—seven women and the rest men, crammed in this truck with no space to move. I sat at the side with my friend. Some were crying because they couldn't move. We didn't know what part of Mexico we were crossing because we couldn't see out of the truck, but it got hotter and we began to have trouble breathing." Fifteen hours after leaving the farm in Chiapas, they were in Puebla, about eighty miles southeast of Mexico City. They stayed there another week. Magali said a child joined them, but when he saw the truck with the hiding place, he called his father, who was living in New York City, and they decided he should go back to Guatemala. "He was crying. We talked to him, let him know we would take care of him, but he wanted to leave."

At night it was bitterly cold, but there weren't enough blankets to go around. On the day they were due to leave the truck arrived at 1:00 A.M. to collect them. It took fifteen hours to get to another town, but even then they were still seventeen hours from the US border. "We were hungry, so I climbed a guava tree to pick fruit for us to share," Magali told me. Shortly afterward she found out that from there they weren't heading to the Texas border at all; instead they would be crossing through the Arizona desert, around eight hundred miles to the west. There was nothing she could do. Her plans had irrevocably changed, and she had no agency over the route her life would take next. "We drove overnight and arrived in Agua Prieta on the border the next morning," she said. "I had never been in the desert, so I had no idea how hot it was going to be. That afternoon we were split into three trucks and told they were going to drop us off in Arizona. The vehicles didn't stop; they were driving slowly, and everybody had to jump out and run into the desert. Then a guide said, 'Welcome to Arizona.'" "Guide" is a euphemism Magali uses for "people-trafficker." Maybe it confers on them some kind of trustworthiness—or at least the hope they can be trusted. She made it to the United States unscathed, after all.

Once she was in Arizona, she figured they'd be walking for only thirty minutes or so until they arrived at an American city, but the desert was a vast, never-ending beige canvas dotted with green-brown ironwood trees and thorny mesquite stretching all the way to the horizon. They were there for three days. The smugglers gave each of them a backpack, inside of which were lemons and some food, like tinned tuna fish, together with two gallons of water. "It started to rain, and my friend and I were crying, thinking the worst would happen," Magali told me. "We were soaking, and the extra clothes we'd picked got wet. That night it was still raining and we began walking—the guide said we couldn't stop because Border Patrol were passing by every five minutes. We heard a coyote howling. Our shoes were slippery, and everyone fell and dropped their water; the bottles got holes in them. We heard rattlesnakes but couldn't see them."

For three nights the group walked, hiding under trees or brush during the day to escape the sun and the eagle eyes of immigration enforcement. They tried to take shifts napping while others kept watch, but it was impossible—Border Patrol helicopters passed overhead, the *chuf chuf chuf* of the rotor blades disrupting any idea of rest. Magali said they watched some of the guides consume drugs; she could smell weed and saw others snort a white powder.

A Guatemalan trafficker said all the women should stay together for protection. Eventually they arrived at a ranch. A Nicaraguan woman had swollen knees from falling on a rock and couldn't go any farther. The men in her group wanted to leave her there. "She held on to me, asking me to help her," Magali said. "She didn't want to die there; she had two children back in Nicaragua. But we couldn't stay with her. My group was leaving, and they were walking fast. We told her she should start a fire so coyotes wouldn't come close to her. I don't know what happened to her."

Eventually Magali and the others emerged from the desert and reached a highway. "We were hiding in the bushes when we heard a boy saying, 'It's ready, the truck is here, run.' It was a van and the seats had been removed. They told the women to climb in first, followed by the men." As the van sped away, one of its tires exploded, and the passengers were made to jump out and hide on a nearby ranch. Magali saw a police vehicle pass by. Her friend was too tired to run anymore; her lips were cracked and bleeding, and they'd run out of water. She isn't sure how, but Magali said the people-traffickers managed to find another vehicle, and a few hours later they were on the road again.

Meanwhile, Magali's friend in Austin wondered why she wasn't in Texas. From the border crossing at Piedras Negras, Magali only had to get across the Rio Grande and into Eagle Pass, and from there it was just a three-and-a-half-hour journey to Austin. Magali told her the guides had taken her to Arizona instead—that her

onward journey was now in the opposite direction; she was heading for California.

It would be three years before Magali would make it to Austin.
In California she worked with various families, cleaning and looking after their children. It was brutal work and she was treated
appallingly, but she was desperate to pay back the money she'd
borrowed. Then, in July 2007, she was finally able to pay a friend in
California $700 to drive her to Austin. When she arrived after a
twenty-hour journey, she wondered how she would move around
the city; in California she'd been able to take the bus everywhere,
she knew all the routes and stops. Her friend in Austin told her
she would have to drive because where she lived there were no
buses, but Magali was anxious that if she got stopped by the police
and they found she didn't have a driver's license, they would
impound the car. She worked with her friend cleaning houses. "I
remember once we were driving to south Austin. A van pulled up
next to us at a traffic light, and my friend noticed the driver had
'ICE' stitched on his shirtsleeve. I told her not to look at him, to
just keep driving."

Magali's future husband used to rent a room in her friend's
house; he told her he saw her when she first arrived in Austin, but
she doesn't remember. Eventually they became friends. They'd
play basketball and soccer together in the neighborhood. Three
years later they got together.

Years before Magali arrived in Austin, the city council had
pondered whether to make the city a safe haven for refugees
from Central America. Back in the late 1980s, then mayor Frank
Cooksey wanted Austin designated a "sanctuary city" but he ultimately couldn't get the support. By the time Magali arrived, there
were several community organizations providing help to undocumented migrants, like Casa Marianella, an interfaith project
that opened in Austin in the mid-'80s to ensure safe housing and
access to services for displaced migrants fleeing Central America,

and the Workers Defense Project, set up to help construction workers secure workplace rights from paid sick leave to humane working conditions. Austin seemed like a welcoming place with the resources to help people like Magali integrate into the community and navigate the challenges of living in the United States without legal status. After all, this was a city that had renamed First Street as Cesar Chavez Street to honor the American labor leader and civil rights activist after his death. Perhaps the fact that renaming the road proved contentious should have been a warning sign, though; the process took several years and involved multiple rounds of public hearings and community input, and it faced opposition from some business owners and residents along the street who thought the change would be costly and disruptive.

In 2001, then governor Rick Perry signed the Texas DREAM Act into law. It was a bipartisan piece of legislation that allowed undocumented immigrants like Magali to be classified as state residents in order for them to pay in-state tuition and attend public colleges and universities. Prior to that they were charged out-of-state or international rates. If you were entirely unaware of Texas politics and found out about the DREAM Act—and subsequently discovered Texas was also the first state in the nation to pass this kind of legislation—you might assume it was an incredibly immigrant-friendly place. But in the years since its passage, the legislature has become more conservative, and legislators have done their damnedest to repeal it, in addition to filing more than one hundred anti-immigrant bills. Just two years after the DREAM Act passed, a new law prevented certain immigrants from obtaining driver's licenses; others granted local police the authority to carry out immigration enforcement and awarded hundreds of millions of dollars in funding for surveillance of—and to bolster policing on—the border.

Magali's son was born in 2011. He was six when Donald Trump was sworn into office. In 2017, the new president spoke of building a wall to keep undocumented immigrants out of America. Republicans in the Senate attempted to pass the RAISE Act with the aim of reducing legal immigration to the United States by 50 percent by halving the number of green cards issued. Trump said he would cap refugee admissions. Because of the anti-immigrant rhetoric sweeping the country, Magali and her husband were afraid they would be deported like some of their friends. "We were so scared, scared to buy groceries," she told me. So Magali and her husband made a plan: if one of them got deported, the other would take care of their son in America. And they would also save money in case they needed to pay for a lawyer to fight repatriation to Guatemala. "My eldest brother told me to write a letter to a friend making it clear that if my husband and I were both deported, we gave permission for our son to stay with that family," she said. Today, when they send their son, who is a US citizen by birth, back to Guatemala to see family, he has to walk into the airport alone.

I'd chosen to live in a place that held me as legitimate but Magali as illegitimate. Our children, both American citizens by virtue of their birth, were afforded the same rights. But not their parents. I'm embarrassed to admit I had no idea what Magali was going through at the time—because I'd never asked her. An estimated fifty thousand Guatemalans were deported from the United States in 2013. They returned to discover a country pretty much unchanged since they left, one beset by violence, where there was too much red tape and few employment opportunities. The Guatemalan government launched several programs to try to help those returning, but it's hard when they faced social stigma; reintegrating was a struggle.

Back in Austin, Magali said interactions with the police are always scary. "We're no longer as afraid to pick up groceries, but we always drive carefully." A couple of years back their landlord increased their rent, so they moved into an RV for a while. They recently relocated to Hutto, thirty miles northeast of Austin, sharing a house with friends. But Magali has no idea how long they'll stay or where they'll go next.

BACK IN 2006, I INTERVIEWED the British film director Nick Broomfield. Known for his unflinching interrogation of his documentary subjects, such as the famous Hollywood madam Heidi Fleiss and the serial killer Aileen Wuornos, Nick had that year turned his attention to drama, working on a film about Chinese immigrants in the UK. The film was called *Ghosts*, and it was inspired by the real-life Morecambe Bay "cockle picker" tragedy. A couple of years earlier, twenty-three undocumented Chinese laborers, trafficked to England via criminal gangs, drowned while picking cockles at night off the Lancashire coast when the tide came in. Nick told me he was interested in the idea of modern slavery: back then three million migrant workers in the UK helped fuel its economy, working in the supply chain, in slaughterhouses and farms, producing food that's sold at rock-bottom prices in grocery stores (today it's more like five million), but nobody benefiting from their labor was taking responsibility for their welfare. They were, Nick said, "mercilessly exploited, receiving less than the minimum wage, working ridiculous hours, and living five to a bedroom."

But that was in my native UK. Having lived in Texas, I'd seen firsthand how the state's government treated undocumented immigrants who, similarly, bolstered its economy. And if anyone in Austin thought the city's progressive credentials extended to ensuring they had shelter and safety, they were mistaken.

THE MIGRATION POLICY INSTITUTE ESTIMATES that today there are 1.8 million undocumented immigrants living in Texas, of which more than a million are employed in the labor force. Study after study has shown that undocumented workers contribute substantially to the state's economy—one estimate puts that figure at $30 billion annually. Back in 2006, the office of Texas's (Republican) state comptroller Carole Keeton Strayhorn conducted what it said was the first comprehensive financial analysis of the impact of undocumented immigrants like Magali on the state's budget and economy. It concluded that if Texas lost what was estimated, back in 2005, to be 1.4 million undocumented immigrants, it would have seen around $17.7 billion in annual gross domestic product that year disappear. Strayhorn's report estimated that undocumented immigrants in Texas generated more taxes and other revenue than the state spent on them. Fast-forward to 2020, and a study by Rice University found that for every dollar the Texas state government spent on public services for undocumented immigrants, it collected $1.21 in revenue.

But this was Texas, and instead of acknowledging the financial, cultural, and other benefits that immigrants brought to the state, in 2017 the legislature passed SB4. Nicknamed the "Show Me Your Papers" law, it was described as one of the most anti-immigrant bills in the country, allowing police to check the immigration status of anyone they arrested and effectively outlawing sanctuary cities—communities that discourage police from reporting an individual's immigration status or honoring requests by ICE to detain undocumented immigrants unless they are investigating a serious crime. After Texas passed SB4, the City of Austin responded with two resolutions aimed at reversing what it saw as some of the law's most toxic properties. The first said if you were stopped for an offense where police could just issue a citation (like speeding, petty theft, or possession of up to four ounces of marijuana), they must then release you. The second required police to advise people of their right to remain silent before asking about their immigration status. As a result, Austin became the first "Freedom City" in Texas, after more than one hundred locals testified in support of the two resolutions, which they said would keep the community safer for immigrants. Austin may have enacted laws designed to keep immigrants safer, but Austin was in Texas, which in turn was making its own laws designed to do the exact opposite. Magali, and thousands of undocumented immigrants like her, were essentially pawns in this game between politicians, the consequences of which were arrest, prison, detention, deportation, separation.

THE LANGUAGE THOSE POLITICIANS USED to talk about migration had real-world consequences. Governor Greg Abbott regularly described migrants crossing the southern border into Texas as an "invasion." Lieutenant Governor Dan Patrick told a Fox News host his state was "being invaded." In 2019, a twenty-one-year-old white man from Dallas drove 630 miles to El Paso, near the Mexican border, where he walked into a crowded Walmart with a semiautomatic rifle and opened fire. He killed twenty-three people that day and wounded twenty-two more—an attack, he wrote, that was "a response to the Hispanic invasion of Texas"; that he was "simply defending [his] country from cultural and ethnic replacement brought on by the invasion." It's the language of white nationalism; it's the language of Trump and of the politicians who supported him. Anti-immigrant rhetoric has become increasingly mainstreamed.

Texas—and Austin—need people like Magali; they are as much Austinites as anyone. Seeing the way in which Magali and her family are forced to live on the outskirts of Austin—in the shadows, in a kind of nonexistence—made me realize that the city wasn't this bucolic place I'd once imagined it was, that politicians can dictate who belongs in a city and who doesn't.

And Texas continues on its rightward path, dragging Austin along with it. In 2021, a Texas judge halted new applications to Texas's Deferred Action for Childhood Arrivals program. Known as DACA, it gave DREAMers the temporary right to live in the United States. Now, they will graduate high school unable to apply for legal status. An estimated 175,000 noncitizens in Austin are potentially at risk of deportation. Ghosts. Just like Magali.

CHAPTER 9

WMD

It took some time, but over the years I lived in Austin, I began to realize that an awful lot of people had guns. A lot of people I knew had them too. But it wasn't until Olive was born in the summer of 2011 that I really gave it much thought, particularly with regard to how it affected us personally.

Texans buy more guns than residents of any other state—more than 1.6 million were sold to Texans in 2021 alone. Guns are inextricably bound up in the mythology of being Texan, and they've played a pivotal role in the state's story—from the famous "Come and Take It" cannon flag raised at the Battle of Gonzales, when Texian settlers fought for independence from Mexico, to the image of the gun-toting Ethan Edwards, played by John Wayne, riding across the west Texas desert in John Ford's western *The Searchers*.

In reality, it wasn't until the late 1990s that the Republican-dominated legislature began turning Texas into a gun-toting state, dismantling what were some fairly stringent and sensible regulations governing weapons that had been enacted over the years since the Wild West era. The Republicans started with a law that allowed Texans to apply for a license to carry concealed pistols in public, setting aside federal gun laws. Some of the impetus for introducing the so-called license to carry came after hearing testimony in the legislature from a woman named Suzanna Hupp.

In 1991, Hupp had been having lunch with her parents at a Luby's Cafeteria in the small town of Killeen, an hour and fifteen minutes north of Austin, when a man plowed his truck through a wall and opened fire with a handgun, killing twenty-three people including Hupp's parents. Hupp's handgun was outside, in her car, and she said if she'd been allowed to carry it into the cafeteria that afternoon, the outcome could have been very different. The law passed, and suddenly anyone in Texas over twenty-one who didn't have a criminal record could take a ten- to fifteen-hour test and then carry a pistol pretty much wherever they wanted as long as it wasn't visible. Then governor George W. Bush called it "a bill to make Texas a safer place." At the time, by the way, you didn't need any kind of license to carry a rifle or shotgun. There was no waiting period to buy one and no registration necessary.

At least in my early years living in Austin, the proliferation of guns didn't feel overwhelming—if, indeed, I thought about it at all. I wrote about American gun culture a fair bit, but as far as pondering what I thought about living in a place where they were everywhere, guns were just an eccentric postscript to conversations with friends and family back home about my life in Texas. Then after Olive was born, I think I sat up and paid attention. Paid attention to the fact that more preschoolers were being gunned down each year in America than police officers in the line of duty.

The truth was, in Texas, guns were ubiquitous and even part of the lexicon of its lawmakers. When officials in Austin were deciding whether to allow gun shows to be hosted at the Travis County Exposition Center, Greg Abbott, who was then serving as the state's attorney general, took to Twitter to say that if the city tried to ban the show, it "better be ready for a double-barreled lawsuit."

BACK IN 1999, SOMEWHERE OUTSIDE of St. Louis, Missouri, on our road trip across the States, Luke and I heard on the car radio about a shooting that had happened at Columbine High School in Colorado. Two twelfth grade students had pulled carbines and semiautomatic pistols from their trench coats and, over the next fifty minutes, had slaughtered twelve students and a teacher. At the time Columbine was the deadliest high school shooting in American history and a gut-punch reality check that we weren't in England anymore. Naively, though, I'd felt safe in Austin—like this shining city we'd just discovered seemed somehow immune to violence like this. But this was Texas, where gun memes like "Texas Is Pro-Choice: Choose Which Gun You Want to Carry" were ubiquitous and, apparently, funny.

By 2009, guns outnumbered people in America, and it wasn't uncommon to hear stories of thwarted shootings. Forrest Preece, who went on to work with Michael Dell and his nascent computer company, had narrowly missed a bullet back in 1966, when the University of Texas became the scene of America's first ever mass school shooting. He told me that sort of thing didn't happen back then. It's what went unsaid that is so profoundly scary: that that sort of thing *does happen now*. It happens all the time.

Shannon and I began wondering about Austin. Becoming a parent has a way of doing that to you, shattering any naïveté you have about the world. All we wanted to do was keep Olive safe. What would happen if, when she started school in a few years, the unthinkable happened? What if the unthinkable was a lot more likely than we'd ever thought? We hadn't remotely imagined leaving Texas—or the United States—before that point, but then the wheels started spinning.

I'D WRITTEN A LOT ABOUT guns and gun violence since moving to Texas, but in the fall of 2012, when Olive was a year old, I bought one for myself. Actually, it was for a story for *GQ* magazine—I wanted to delve into the world of American gun ownership but also find out why anyone would feel the need to own one, particu-larly in a laid-back, supposedly progressive city like Austin. Even as a new parent, fearful for my child, I thought maybe shootings were more anomalies than anything else—maybe we didn't have so much to worry about? Regardless, I wouldn't keep the gun in the house; I'd store it in the garage, which wasn't connected, and after I finished writing the story, I'd get rid of it.

My FBI background check lasted about five minutes over the phone, and, at the gun store, I checked the relevant boxes on a form headed "Firearms Transaction Record" that assured the shop I wasn't addicted to any drug, nor had I ever been "adjudi-cated as a mental defective." In the story I subsequently wrote for British *GQ*, I noted that, driving back to my house with the gun on the passenger seat, it occurred to me I didn't know how to load it, let alone fire it. Where I'm from in England, the only guns re-ally are shotguns for pheasant and skeet shooting. My dad has one, and the law says it must be locked up in a safe that's bolted to the wall, with the keys kept in a separate location. Even the regular cops on the beat don't carry guns. And guess what: we don't have an epidemic of gun violence over there.

I envisaged using my experience as a gun owner in Austin as a device to tell a wider story about gun ownership more generally in America, but the story took a turn when a couple of months after I bought my pistol, a twenty-year-old man in Connecticut executed twenty children and six staff members at an elementary school. All the children killed at Sandy Hook were between six and seven years old, and the tragedy overwhelmed me. I ached for the par-ents who'd lost their children, who were dealing with people like Alex Jones pretending that it wasn't a massacre.

And I felt, personally, terrified. My wife and I had chosen to raise Olive in a country that, quite frankly, had a problem with gun violence—and in a state that in a decade would see more mass shootings than any other. I could no longer bury my head in the sand. I wanted to know, statistically, how safe we were, and how safe our daughter would be when she started school in a place that seemed to value the freedom to own a gun over the freedom to go to that school without the fear of being mown down. Meanwhile, arguing that in the wake of the Sandy Hook massacre more people should carry concealed handguns, the brother of one of my wife's friends wrote on Facebook, "Think of it like having a bunch of off-duty policemen walking around." What was the right move? What was the safe one?

The governor of Texas at the time was Rick Perry. Three days after the Newtown shooting he warned against a "knee-jerk reaction" from the federal government and managed to elicit applause when he mentioned one school in Texas that already allowed staff members to carry guns. At the time, you could apply for a concealed handgun license, which I did and which enabled me to carry my weapon pretty much anywhere except a post office, a school, or within a thousand feet of a prison on the day it's carrying out an execution. Texas lawmakers would ultimately do away with those restrictions altogether, and in 2021, it would become legal for anyone over twenty-one without a conviction to carry a handgun in most public places without a license.

For the story, I practiced shooting my gun at a local range in Austin and also took turns on a Glock 9mm and .45, a .22 Ruger, a .357 Smith & Wesson, a .38 six-shooter, a Kimber .45, and a Walther PPK. I also attended a ten-hour class on gun safety, took a shooting test, and learned when I could use it against another human being. Texas has a Stand Your Ground law, which means you can use your weapon to defend against an intruder in your home (or car) if your life is being threatened. My instructor told us, "Every bullet has an attorney's name on it." He also told me I could take my gun into a bank (for the most part), adding, "It sometimes helps withdrawals go a little quicker." I could also carry it, loaded, into the Texas state capitol downtown if I wanted. In fact, there's a separate entrance just for gun owners, at which a state trooper checks your license. Today, because anyone can carry a gun without a license, the trooper is there just to "vet" you before you walk in. For the *GQ* story I loaded my Sig with bullets and went in. An officer in a cowboy hat ran my permit through a computer, and within seconds I was inside the capitol. Meanwhile, my photographer friend Matt Rainwaters, who was chronicling the experience for the magazine and didn't have a handgun permit of his own, had his pockets searched and had to run his bag through the X-ray machine.

HANDGUN LICENSE HOLDERS WERE GENERALLY well-behaved, and the statistics kept by the Texas Department of Public Safety seemed to back that up: of the 63,679 convictions in Texas in 2011, just 120 were committed by license holders. My instructor told me if one was ever pulled over by the police for speeding, the tension would just "dissolve" once officers discovered they were dealing with a handgun license holder. I wasn't convinced, so I began asking police officers on the beat in Austin what they thought. The responses I got were, variously, "no," "not at all," and laughter. One told me he'd want to see both my hands on my car window and that he'd ask for my gun and keep it in his vehicle for the duration of the traffic stop. "If anything, I'm more tense because I know you've got a gun," he said. Another described a frightening scenario in which he could be called to the scene of a shooting only to find a license holder had already begun to engage the attacker with his own weapon. How could a police officer, anxious, heart racing, distinguish between a "good guy with a gun" and a "bad guy with a gun"? I discovered that the pro-gun brigade will have you believe that the police love concealed handgun license holders. They don't. What's more, I found that concealed handgun license holders were mostly middle-class white men who wanted to defend against people they perceived as dangerous—which meant especially men of an ethnic minority.

A gun-owning friend told me about an incident that happened outside a house in east Austin. A man had begun peeing on his friend's washer/dryer that he had temporarily stored outside. His friend confronted him, and the man pulled a gun. His friend pulled a gun too, and the pair froze. No shots were fired, no one got hurt, and the man left. But my friend was convinced, after this, that he needed to keep a gun on his bedside table and another in his car from then on. The story he told me was all the proof he needed. Most gun owners I spoke to said they wanted them for protection, but I struggled to see what they needed protecting from. A washer/dryer urinator, perhaps?

For the *GQ* story I submitted an open records request to the Austin Police Department and found that in a city that in 2013 (when the story was published) had a population of 820,000, it had an average of just eighty-two "home invasions" a year. And in the five years leading up to 2013, only one person had been killed in one of those burglaries—the information I got from the police didn't specify whether that was the homeowner or the burglar. I did discover that during that half decade, though, Austin had seen three accidental shooting deaths and sixty-nine accidental shooting injuries. That chimed with a study published in 1998 that showed guns kept in American homes were twenty-two times more likely to be used in unintentional shootings, murder, assault, or suicide attempts than for self-defense. And it's just getting worse.

In 2020, the Centers for Disease Control recorded the highest number of gun-related deaths ever, and today guns are the leading cause of death among young people in the United States. That year, Texas saw 4,164 gun deaths—14.2 per 100,000 people, more than died in road traffic accidents. That's astonishing. Texas falls somewhere in the middle of gun deaths and road traffic deaths in the United States, but the fact that gun deaths outnumber road traffic deaths is frightening. We used to use car deaths as a metric to smooth the way for other seemingly risky endeavors. Nervous about a plane journey? Car rides are far more dangerous. Worried about taking the train across the country? Far safer than driving. Worried about being shot? . . .

In Austin, particularly, gun violence is rising, but it's easy to be lulled into a false sense of security that gun deaths and injuries just don't happen there. It's Austin, after all. Peace-loving, progressive Austin. The fact is, though, the Texas legislature has made it dead easy to buy a gun anywhere in Texas without going through any hoops at all. If you're over twenty-one and haven't been convicted of a felony, you can just pop into Academy Sports + Outdoors, like I did for the *GQ* story, and pick up a handgun or semiautomatic rifle. And, like me when I bought my 9mm pistol, you can do it with no idea at all how to use it.

After living in Austin for a while, and particularly after I'd experienced owning a gun, I realized that there's a tendency for new Texans to want to assimilate. Buy the cowboy boots, own the gun. Not because you particularly need to, but because this is Texas and you can. And what's more, you can justify it to your liberal friends and relatives back home in California or wherever by saying it's just for self-defense.

But here's the thing: while you're not going to need a gun to defend yourself against someone breaking into your home at night armed to the teeth, you're best not buying one to defend yourself anywhere else in the city either. Between 2003, the year I moved there, and 2021, the year after I left, there were 297 accidental shooting injuries in Austin.

OLIVE WAS ALMOST THREE YEARS old when we started to seriously entertain the idea of moving back to England. Austin was changing, yes, but the economy and closure of live music venues weren't reason, for us, to leave. After all, we'd put down roots in the city, bought a house, established lifelong friendships, and daydreamed of raising Olive there—our little Texan.

But we couldn't get past the guns. The thought of her going to school in a place where the politicians in charge didn't value those little lives was too much to shoulder.

In the spring of 2014, at 2:39 P.M. one weekday, an email popped into both Shannon's and my inboxes. It was from the head of Olive's day care. "The school is on lockdown until further notice," she wrote. "If you have any questions or concerns feel free to call or email me. Thank you."

Of course we had fucking questions and concerns. I felt my face go red as I shouted to Shannon in the other room, "What the fuck are we doing here in this fucking state?" We tried calling the school, but there was no answer. Twenty minutes passed. Another email landed in our inboxes. "Your child's safety is important to us. We are still currently under a lockdown due to an outside event. We are all okay and I will continue to keep you posted." At times like this, Shannon's usually calmer than I am, but right now she was panicked; our baby was involved in a lockdown—in a day care at that, a supposed sanctuary—and we had no idea what was happening and were helpless. We turned on the local TV news and saw that police had surrounded an apartment complex across the road because of a "domestic incident" involving a man with a gun. We jumped in the car and headed to the school. The building wasn't some fortress—it was the back of a church, and we knew if anyone really wanted to get in there they could. But all we could do was wait for what seemed like an agonizingly long time until it was over.

A month later, I wrote a story about how the Sandy Hook shootings had resulted in more, not less, Americans buying guns. I'd driven to Harlingen in south Texas, near the Mexican border, to attend a pro–Second Amendment rally and found myself in a sea of about a hundred people (mostly men, but some women) with AR-15s slung over their shoulders, surrounded by flags with a picture of a rattlesnake and the words "Don't Tread on Me"—a throwback from the American Revolutionary War—listening to speakers take their turns rallying attendees to protest what they felt were unnecessary restrictions imposed by the government (both local and national) that were infringing on their constitutional right to bear arms. One woman, Angela Pena, a mother holding an M6 rifle, told me she'd never been politically active, but "over the last year I've seen a more and more tyrannical government. You can't pick and choose how much of the Second Amendment you want. My father [fought for his country], and we've always had weapons in our family. It's a tradition and it's part of being an American." Once, Pena said, she was being followed by a man in a parking lot in Austin. She figured he was about to assault or rob her, so she drew her handgun. She didn't have to pull the trigger, she said, as the man ran away. "My father's sacrifices were not in vain. These were the rights they bled and died for."

Another person at the rally told me that he really didn't want to have to openly carry his AR-15s and AK-47s: "It's a burden. It's much easier to exercise our rights with a 9mm." He thought it was crazy that in Texas he could openly carry an assault-style rifle downtown without passing any kind of test or applying for a license, but not a handgun. I thought it was crazy you could do that too, but not for the same reasons he did. But in just a few years he would get his wish, enjoying a Texas in which he no longer had to take a test to get a license and could carry that sidearm openly in a holster.

In the handful of weeks I'd been working on the story, there had been thirteen school shootings in America, and this was at the forefront of our minds when we decided to move to England in the summer of 2014. The fact we chose to do it in the middle of August undoubtedly helped our mental game too—gun culture in

Texas was nuts, and so was the extreme weather. We cleared out our house, sold a load of furniture and put the rest in storage, and paid an ungodly amount of money to ship everything else to the UK. We were moving for good, we thought, although we wouldn't sell our house in Austin—we'd rent it out, more because we thought it would be a wise investment than a hedge in case we changed our minds later on.

We signed a year's lease on a house that was built in the mid-sixteenth century. It was a three-bedroom thatched building—a chocolate box cottage that, being English, I was fairly used to seeing. Shannon, meanwhile, thought it looked like something out of Lord of the Rings. Its doorframes were certainly built for Hobbits, as the semipermanent lump on the crown of my scalp could attest. The problem was its owners hadn't really updated anything since the 1980s, and as winter came hard and fast to Cambridgeshire, it forced icy gusts of air through our window frames—gusts with which the giant, smoky inglenook fireplace that dominated the living room just couldn't compete. The tiny, picturesque village we'd chosen was a bit boring too: small c conservative and gossipy. The most sensible thing to have done would have been to relocate to a different town after our lease was up.

Instead, a few weeks into living in our new home, we decided we would move back to Austin in a year. Perhaps we were suffering a weird bout of amnesia when it came to the things that had begun to turn us off Austin. I think maybe I'd managed to compartmentalize any fears I had when it came to gun violence, put them in the back of my mind. Perhaps those fears were outsized anyway. Instead we rationalized returning by telling ourselves we had a nice house there, that we loved our neighbors and had good friends nearby, and that Olive would go to school with kids she knew.

To compound the feeling that we'd made a mistake choosing to live where we had in England, our house was robbed that

Christmas. We came back to our dark cottage from dinner one evening around 8:00 P.M. to see burglars in our bedroom through the
window. As we stood on the grass outside, me holding on to Olive,
they ran down the stairs and came out of the broken window they'd
entered through, one of them wielding a pitchfork. He dropped
it in front of us, and they both took off down the road running.
While I've no doubt that if this had been Texas they would have
been armed with guns, we'd already convinced ourselves we'd be
somehow happier moving back. Austin had this intoxicating effect;
there was something overwhelming pulling us back—at least back
then. Either way, twelve months after we had moved to England
forever, we were packing up our stuff again, securing Scruff a spot
in the pressurized hold of a 747, and saying a teary goodbye to my
poor parents, Texas-bound once more. Into the belly of the beast.

We were happy to be home, of course, but the fear hadn't been
alleviated. In fact, concealed carry laws made it, in many ways,
scarier.

Back in 2011, I'd interviewed Angela Stroud, who was studying
for a PhD at the University of Texas and had spent years research-
ing the social meanings of concealed handgun licensing. She had
interviewed scores of people and, like me, had taken the handgun
license test herself so she'd be more informed. She'd found that
the two camps—those opposed to guns and those pro-gun—were
divided between those whose worldview considered what's best
for society and those whose worldview considered what's best for
themselves. With the Second Amendment folks, Angela said, "there
is a major privileging of the individual . . . and it's a powerful
experience to become enmeshed in this worldview. They see two
major threats: one is a criminal who wants to kill you; the other is a
government that wants to control you." Angela ended up writing
a book about how race, class, and gender shaped people's decision
to get their concealed carry permits. It came as little surprise to find
that middle-class white men were most likely to get their licenses

and that they were mostly motivated by a desire to protect their wives and children and to defend against people they perceived as dangerous. In 2004, the National Academy of Sciences conducted a review of the available data and found "no credible evidence that right-to-carry laws decrease or increase violent crime."

I caught up with Angela again a decade later, and she told me in the years since we'd spoken the culture around gun ownership in the United States had been changing. Historically, liberals had not owned guns in large numbers, but since 2012—which is when Angela left Austin—there had been an increase in women and people of color buying guns. Then the Trump era, she told me, changed how people who identified as politically progressive thought about guns. Before that, she said, "liberals were still kind of freaked out by the idea that people walk around with guns." Then there was a big sea change where they began to say, "Okay, now it's commonplace, what does that mean for me?" Angela said that seeing the kind of violence and the threats of violence—this kind of Civil War discourse—led a growing number of progressive people in general, but particularly men, to think that obtaining a gun for self-defense and for defending their family was a good idea. So what about Austin? Angela attributes gun ownership there to this sense of southern masculinity—"Bros going to the gun range . . . to be a man is to be able to defend your family," she told me.

Perhaps it was the job I did, which for a number of years meant writing about gun violence, but I was acutely aware of how pro-lific it was and its impact on victims, their families, and society. I knew the statistics, but I also knew a lot of people who owned guns and their justification for it. There was an emotional reaction to all this too, exacerbated by having brought a small child into the world. The fact that firearms exceeded motor vehicle crashes as the leading cause of injury-related death for people aged one to twenty-four was such a horrific scenario that I couldn't help thinking about it, particularly each time we were told Olive's pre-K had gone through a lockdown drill. It had been only a little more than a year since she'd had to go through a lockdown for real after some asshole with a handgun helped chip away at the innocence of a school full of infants and toddlers.

BACK IN 2013, ART ACEVEDO, Austin's then police chief, told me Austin was a big city with a small-town mentality. Although he kept ringing the alarm that it was no longer a sleepy college town, he says it largely fell on deaf ears. He thinks Austin lost its innocence the day the Yogurt Shop Murders happened. This was 1991, and it cast a dark shadow on the city, not least because they still haven't caught the perpetrators. On the night of December 6, four teenage girls working at an I Can't Believe It's Yogurt! shop in northwest Austin were shot in the head, and at least one raped. The murderer then set the shop alight before fleeing from a back door. In the intervening years there have been false confessions, wrongful imprisonment, and overturned convictions. At the dawn of 2022, investigators said new DNA technology offered hope of finally solving the case. Judy Maggio Rosenfeld, who back then was an anchor for Austin's KVUE news, was on maternity leave when the murders took place. Three decades on she posted on Facebook: ". . . it's hard to comprehend 30 years has passed since the murders changed our city forever. My newborn daughter is now 30. Jennifer [Harbison], Sarah [Harbison], Amy [Ayers] and Eliza [Thomas] would be middle-aged women, likely with families of their own. Austin is a different place than it was in 1991, when the community rallied around these families, held vigils, put up billboards and offered reward money. But I want to believe the heart and soul of our city are the same, and we would still envelop the families with our collective love and dedication if the murders happened today."

Since the murders, the city has experienced explosive growth, but Acevedo reckons that the city council has failed to prioritize public safety. "A shooting in downtown Austin in the entertainment district was absolutely a rare occasion," he said. "Now it seems like there's a shooting every weekend." By 2020, the police budget amounted to $434 million. But that year, bolstered by the "defund the police" movement, the city council unanimously voted to cut its police budget by a third after reform advocates demanded the council spend part of those funds on social services and housing instead. "Good criminal justice reform that is thoughtful can be really good," Acevedo told me, "but I think in Austin the council just took the city backward. To borrow a phrase from the police commissioner in Baltimore, you don't tear down the current stadium until you build the new one."

Austin's efforts to "defund the police" lasted only a year. An analysis by the *Statesman* newspaper found that the council failed to anticipate the consequences of stripping the budget: by 2021, the department was left "with a bare-bones patrol staff suffering unprecedented attrition" and a slower response to 911 calls. The Texas legislature, in turn, enacted legislation barring cities in the state from decreasing their police budgets, and in 2022, Austin boosted police spending by 50 percent to a sizable $443 million.

But behind the "defund the police" movement were legitimate concerns about racial profiling, police brutality, and the deaths of Black people in custody. The movement was nationwide, but "progressive Austin" was not blameless. In the time I'd been living in the city, there were numerous incidents. In 2003, a grand jury that had indicted an Austin police officer for criminally negligent homicide in the fatal shooting of a Black man that summer said residents of east Austin's minority communities were subject to a "different brand of law enforcement." In the six years prior to that, eleven people had died at the hands of Austin police, all but one of them either Black or Hispanic. In 2013, Austinites at a tense town hall meeting called on Art Acevedo to resign after the fatal police shooting of Larry Jackson Jr., who was killed while running away from a detective. Jackson Jr. was the sixth Black man to be fatally shot by Austin police since 2007; Acevedo told those at the meeting to tell people not to run from the police.

Acevedo has also been outspoken about another political hot potato he thinks is causing more crime and more trouble for the police: guns. "The answer to any problem in Texas too often is more guns, making them easier to get. But the more guns you have, the more gun crime you're going to have," he told me. "We have a proliferation of firearms in this state. We make it easier for people to carry firearms, and we make it harder for police officers to actually keep the American people safe. In Austin we have people walking around downtown with an AK-47 legally, with two thirty-round clips—a banana clip where you can tape 'em together and have sixty rounds very quickly. How does that make sense to anybody? It makes no sense, and I think that it's created a huge problem, not only in Austin but in Texas and across our country."

I WAS IN THE MIDDLE of writing yet another story about guns when Parkland happened. By now Olive was a first grader at an elementary school downtown, and it hit home more than I could have imagined, even knowing our fear was always close to heart. Families had moved to Parkland for its neighborhoods and good schools; it was one of the safest cities in Florida, and a former mayor said life there revolved around its open spaces and fields. But on Valentine's Day 2018, nineteen-year-old Nikolas Cruz changed all that after marching into Marjory Stoneman Douglas High School, pulling a Smith & Wesson M&P15 semiautomatic rifle out of his backpack, and firing at students.

Seventeen people dead in just six minutes and twenty seconds. The morning after, Shannon sat in the office at the front of our house emailing Olive's principal to ask how she planned to keep the students safe. "We agonize about sending our only child into a setting where she can be the victim of gun violence," she wrote. "It's heartbreaking and we feel powerless." She asked about active-shooter drills on campus and what was being done to protect the school. Meanwhile, I was in the other room in the throes of writing another story about mass shootings, Facebook messaging with a man, then in his twenties, who eleven years earlier had taken his stepfather's bolt-action rifle and three boxes of cartridges to his high school, stood in the tall grass in a nearby field, and fired into a classroom.

The problem was, in Texas at least, it didn't feel like anything was going to change as far as keeping our kids safe. To most, Austin may have felt like a bubble, protected from the evil facets of American culture, but it wasn't. And I knew that. Even the actor Matthew McConaughey, who would later flirt with the idea of running for governor of Texas and seemed popular with liberals, libertarians, and conservatives alike, was wed to the Second Amendment. After yet another school shooting he wrote, "I believe that responsible, law-abiding Americans have a Second Amendment right, enshrined by our founders, to bear arms. I also believe we have a cultural obligation to take steps toward slowing down the senseless killing of our children."

"Slowing down"? What about stopping it alto-fucking-gether?

McConaughey didn't like the term "gun control," which he described as a "mandate that can infringe on our right," and he thought there should be an age restriction placed on anyone wanting to buy an AR-15, which he described as "the weapon of choice for mass murderers." That age restriction? Twenty-one. If Austin's cheery, mellow, unofficial mascot McConaughey wasn't backing gun restrictions, it was a sign we weren't about to see less gun violence anytime soon.

I knew other people who had left Austin, convinced it was the right move, only to return a year or two later. I think it's easy to develop selective amnesia when you move away from a place you've grown tired of; you forget those compelling, motivating factors that demanded you move in the first place, and instead the rose-tinted and highly selective movie compilation of all the best scenes plays in a loop in your mind. I think that's what happened to me when we decided to move back to Austin after only a year away: *The weather's not really that bad. I miss swimming in the lakes, those lazy afternoons floating in the river drinking Shiner with my Texas pals. And the gun thing? Is it really that bad?*

CHAPTER 10

CHANGES

I n 2008, fresh from his $30 million trip on a Russian rocket to the International Space Station, Austin computer games entrepreneur Richard Garriott told me that from the window of the Soyuz spacecraft he'd been able to make out clearly airplane contrails, the wakes of ships as they maneuvered in and out of harbors, and even major roadways, bridges, and farms beneath him. It takes just ninety minutes for a Soyuz to orbit Earth, and Garriott was able to see a sunrise or sunset every forty-five minutes. When Earth was dark, he said, Austin and San Antonio appeared as two large smatterings of light, fairly close together—a gap that would only become narrower in the future. The two cities may have been separated by around eighty miles of highway, but at some point, looking down from above, they would blur into a single smudge of bright light, their simultaneous sprawl of real estate and traffic shrinking the distance between them and merging them into a single megalopolis. But it's not just the cities that are blurring together as they expand outward. The cities themselves are becoming homogenized: the little stores, bodegas, and cafés are being uprooted, replaced by chain stores with their familiar bland signage. The suburban strip mall is taking over the inner city.

AUSTIN WAS KNOWN FOR ITS independent shops, quirky bars, music venues, and homegrown restaurants. Want Walmart,

Chick-fil-A, Red Lobster, or Applebee's? You'd find them on the outskirts of town or off the highways. But in 2017, residents on Austin's east side woke up to a huge red-and-white banner wrapped around an iconic but abandoned building on Sixth and Waller Streets that once housed a butcher shop, bakery, and bar. The Uptown Sports Club, with its huge red lettering and faded wood walls daubed in graffiti and band posters, had become part of the furniture of east Austin and was heading for federal historic landmark status. But that morning, people on their commute or on their way to pick up their first coffee of the day were stopped in their tracks. A sign on the old building that had evidently gone up overnight read: "Fall 2017. Chili's East," complete with an image of a red pepper in between the *ea* and *st*. On another side of the building it said: "There's a new king on the east side" and "The classics never go out of style."

The east side was undergoing considerable changes, to be sure. Condos were going up, quiet neighborhoods were getting noisier, and fancy restaurants were opening. But was Sixth and Waller really about to get a popular chain restaurant known for its chicken wings and bacon ranch quesadillas? The signage also pointed to an Instagram account, where one post read: "IT'S FRY-DAY! Tell the kids to put down their fidget spinners and find your way to #ChilisEastATX where you can fill up with our festive Fun Fun Fun Fries" (a play on the Austin festival Fun Fun Fun Fest). The post ended with the hashtags: #fall2017, #Fryday, #EatAuthentic, and #EastAustinOriginal.

A Chili's opening on East Sixth was unthinkable to some but not all that surprising. Others didn't believe it—even a rapidly changing Austin wouldn't allow that. A TV station carried out vox pops with some locals. One woman, who thought it was all a hoax, said it certainly screamed, "Look what might happen here." When the media asked Chili's to wade in, the company tweeted, "That would be weird for us to move to East 6th. #KeepAustinWeird

#FakeNews." Most people saw the prank as an effort to spur a debate around gentrification on the east side. It even won the *Austin Chronicle*'s critics' pick for Most Like No Prank Else at the annual Best of Austin awards that year. "Banners, posters, and a social media push announcing the opening of a Chili's on East Sixth and Waller had locals up in arms about the gentrification and overzealous development of our dear city," the paper said. "With Austin City Limitless Queso, Waller Wings, and Fun Fun Fun Fries on the signature menu, it was just too much to take. Turns out, this doomsday scenario was merely a clever (and not-inexpensive) prank masterminded by an anonymous collective."

That "anonymous collective" was actually a designer friend of mine, Cody Haltom, and a pal of his, who had struck upon the idea for the fake Chili's to foster more conversation about what was happening to the east side. "It's wild—that prank was years ago and felt like a clear joke," he told me. "Now a Chili's could go in that area and nobody would blink. They already have a Target, Whole Foods, Spectrum, and Chipotle there." Occasionally, in order to highlight the absurdity or the painful or negative ramifications of something that's plaguing you or your community, you can gain more traction and be more impactful if you do it through humor.

Ironically, though, that "doomsday scenario," as the *Chronicle* called it, has all but come to pass. For some time now, those big-box retailers, so long a feature of out-of-town highways, have been making their move into cities. Target introduced "urban Targets," some as small as twelve thousand square feet; Walmart launched Walmart Neighborhood Markets; and Ikea kicked off Ikea Planning Studios. Today, our cities are becoming cookie-cutter versions of our suburbs, and when this happens—when cities become homogenized—they lose those unique cultures and histories of the people who live or lived in them; cities become indistinguishable from one another, just places playing host to the same stores, condos, restaurants, and sterile office parks.

Generic. Soulless. Less diverse and vibrant. And because of that, the people who call them home are less likely to feel connected to any kind of community.

THANKFULLY UPTOWN SPORTS CLUB NEVER became a Chili's. It would eventually be turned into a bar and coffee shop courtesy of Austin barbecue entrepreneur Aaron Franklin. But of course having a Chili's in the neighborhood isn't the real problem. Nor is having a Target that displaced an old music venue. As my friend Kevin Ashton told me, that kind of change is systemic and is the inevitable result of free-market capitalism. The only way to oppose that kind of change is to oppose free-market capitalism, which, as Kevin pointed out, most Americans don't want to do.

Kevin's responsible for coining the term "Internet of Things," the idea that it's not just computers that can be hooked up to the internet but physical devices, vehicles, buildings, and more, all of which will revolutionize manufacturing and medicine and re-imagine cities in the future. Today Kevin writes popular science books, and when you get him on a roll predicting what's ahead for all of us, it's fascinating. Kevin reckons if we insist on having an unregulated market where everything goes to the highest bidder, we're going to see a Starbucks on every corner, and that'll happen, he says, "because everybody buys fucking Starbucks." By the same token, if enough people shop at the Walmart that apparently no-body wanted in the neighborhood in the first place, he says it's going to stay there. What we're really saying is we don't want a place for *those* people to go. And so this kind of homogenization is the inevitable result of a system that most people think they like. "Saying 'I used to love Joe's coffee shop that my friend Joe ran but it's now a Starbucks' is privileged hand-wringing at its finest," Kevin says. "Like that's really the thing that you're worried about?"

The things people are really worrying about when they worry about gentrification are way down the list of what should really matter. What should matter is the fact it's impossible to have a city where everybody makes above-average wages, and what we do instead is push certain people into longer and longer commutes, into neighborhoods that will be food deserts until they flip too and become gentrified—or, as Kevin puts it, "until Whole Foods decides it wants to be there." Right now, he says, you don't have to go very far outside of Austin to find communities that are five miles from the nearest grocery store. And they're five miles from the nearest bus stop too. They are home to the folks who work in the kitchens of the restaurants we love to patronize, who clean our houses for fifteen bucks an hour, who keep the streets clean. And as those streets become choked with more traffic and they're forced farther and farther out because of the rise in property prices, rents, and taxes, what hope do they have of Austin ever doing anything to address the problem? Has the proverbial train already left the station?

"There is no train," Kevin says. But he adds that it's never too late; the problem is there's not enough political will to invest in a proper subway system, and in every referendum there's always been opposition to expanding infrastructure because people don't want their taxes to go up. Kevin points to London's Tube network as an example of how public transport can democratize a city, how a huge piece of infrastructure constructed in Victorian times has proved to be a remarkable investment for the future and has enabled the city to keep growing.

As long as you employ short-term thinking, you're going to have a city that works only for some of its population. In a decade, Austin could come to resemble Los Angeles, with unimaginable traffic, because it's pushing more and more people out. And it's not just poor people. Kevin says if you're making $100,000 working for a tech firm, and you and your partner are about to have kids and want them to grow up in a house where they've each got a bedroom and there's a yard to play in, unless you're a millionaire you've got to move out of Austin. And so you'll make a choice to live in the suburbs or in another town, which, at rush hour, is at least an hour's commute from downtown. So yes, your kids will have a yard to play in, but they won't get to see you very much, which will inevitably take a toll on your and their quality of life. Kevin's prediction is pretty dark: long commutes, decaying infrastructure, family stress.

But I think it's pretty accurate. It's already happening. My neighborhood, cheap when we moved in, got so much more expensive in the decade we owned there. We'd never have been able to buy our house at 2019, let alone post-pandemic, prices. We'd bought our home for $165,000 in 2010; it was hard to find anything under $600,000 in 2021—and most went to people willing to pay over the asking price. Property taxes skyrocketed too. We knew several families who sold up and moved farther out—to Round Rock, Pflugerville. And today those places they moved to are unaffordable for a lot of people too. "For the millionaires that can afford to live in Austin today," Kevin says, "ten years from now they'll need to be multimillionaires. And all the nice places in the city will be vacant fifty weeks of the year because the person who bought that million-dollar penthouse only wants to use it for SXSW each March. If your only solution to that is to build another toll road, which is apparently the Texas way, you're fucked."

After we said our goodbyes that day, Kevin texted me a photograph of a city skyline and told me if I showed it to someone who'd been to Austin and told them it was Austin, they'd believe me. "But it's not," he messaged me. "It's Wuhan in China." We were two years into the pandemic, which is why Kevin had chosen that city, but it could have been anywhere of a similar size; that was his point. And he was right. Sure, there are certain angles from which you can look at Austin and it's unmistakably Austin, such as the small stretch of

I-35 where you can spot the capitol and the UT Tower, but from most vantage points it doesn't look anything like the city I'd left just a year and a half before Kevin texted me that picture. It was completely different. But more profoundly, today it could be any city at all; its skyline interchangeable with other cities of the same size.

BY THE TIME I MOVED to Austin, it was already experiencing phenomenal growth. It's just that it wasn't glaringly obvious as you drove around town. After Rick Perry became governor in 2000, he ensured Texas dished out more per year in incentives and subsidies to companies than any other state—over $19 billion a year as a sweetener to lure them to Texas or expand their in-state operations. In Austin this included $232 million in grants, loans, and tax refunds to Samsung, $40 million to Sematech, and almost $30 million to Apple.

Of course, I noticed *some* signs the city had growing pains. In the spring of 2004, Shannon and I went to see David Bowie play at the Backyard, an outdoor music venue in the rolling hills forty minutes west of downtown. It was surrounded by cedar trees, and that night there was a chill in the air. We stood in front of a huge live oak that dominated the back of the venue but could still see stars through its branches. On the stage, Bowie launched into "The Man Who Sold the World." It was an unforgettable experience in a unique venue that, in some ways, was so typical of Austin in the early 2000s. It was inconvenient to get to, and there was little in the way of food nearby, but an outdoor venue in the middle of nowhere offered an experience so idiosyncratic I knew I'd never forget that night. Back then, entrepreneurial Austinites seemed motivated more by what they thought would be a cool addition to the city, by what people would like than what would make them tons of money. A few years on, developers would build a strip mall around the Backyard to house chain stores.

Fast-forward to November 2021, and Mick Jagger, in Austin with the Rolling Stones to play at Circuit of the Americas, the sprawling new home of Formula One, posted a photo on his Instagram account of him sipping a beer outside the Broken Spoke, an old-time country music hall that has stood in the same place on South Lamar Boulevard since 1964. The photo was tightly cropped—you could see the neon sign above him, the wooden walls of the venue, and two "spokes" in the fencing outside. But if you'd been able to zoom out, you'd have seen that the same thing had happened to the Spoke as the Backyard: it was now surrounded by newly built offices and apartments. I struggle to think of a more visceral example of the changes I'd seen taking place in Austin while I lived there than when I saw the Backyard absorbed by a strip mall. Soon it would happen all around town.

OFTEN CONVERSATIONS ABOUT GENTRIFICATION FOCUS entirely on people and not place. But when old buildings with character are torn down and replaced by new, nondescript buildings, cities can lose their sense of identity. Old buildings often have history and culture baked into their walls.

By the mid-2000s, as Austin's skyline was changing and the city growing, so too was the SXSW festival; it was like there was some kind of symbiosis happening, which saw the festival's growth mimicking that of the city that hosted it. In 2010, for the first time since it launched in 1994, SXSW Interactive—a separate festival devoted to the tech industry—announced that its attendance figures had surpassed those of the music festival. SXSW again reflected the city as a whole: big tech had taken over Austin (again). Austin was now Austin 2.0, and as if to illustrate it perfectly, when Dolly Parton made her SXSW debut in 2022, her performance was, as one music writer so perfectly put it, "the creamy filling of a night-long blockchain commercial." Of course, after those two weeks in

March each year the city empties out and things invariably return to normal. But since I'd been living in Austin, I'd witnessed that "normal" change. It's not SXSW's fault outright that rent, property prices, and property taxes were spiraling out of control, but the repercussions of that growth for ordinary Austinites was profound.

WHEN GREG ABBOTT TOOK OVER the reins of the state from Rick Perry in 2015, he continued what Perry had started, enticing Oracle and Charles Schwab to Austin. Between 2011 and 2015, revenue from hotel room bookings grew by 60 percent, topping a billion dollars in 2015. It looked like the entire city was under construction—and it was happening so quickly it was as if these gigantic blue, red, and yellow steel cranes that towered over Austin were in fact 3D printers, spitting out hotels, office blocks, and condos overnight.

AT 10:00 A.M. ONE WEEKDAY in early 2022, I stood at the corner of Sixth and Guadalupe Streets, staring at a small, single-story yellow brick house designed in the Greek Revival style with white pillars that supported a porch along the front. On one side, some of its guttering was falling off. The pitch of the street meant that at some point in the distant past its occupants would have had an unobstructed view of the river, half a mile to the south. Limbs of the few trees that remained in its perimeter stretched toward the road and the only available light. The house constitutes the southern portion of what's known as the Bremond Block Historic District—a cluster of eleven historic mansions and more modest homes that were built sometime between the 1850s and 1910—named after early Austin merchant John Bremond Sr. The house at Sixth and Guadalupe is the James T. Brown House, built in 1855 and one of the oldest of the

Bremond homes. I stood on the sidewalk close to the house, trying to ignore the traffic and construction noise for a minute or
two and picture what Austin once looked like not long after its
founding. It was hard, though: a few yards away a construction
elevator whizzed a slab of concrete skyward, and it was tough
to tell which direction the shrill sound of sawing metal, the buzz
of a drill, and the incessant hammering were coming from. It
became even harder to imagine this house standing in the Austin of the 1800s because towering above it was a sixty-six-story
skyscraper.

At the time I was there the high-rise was still under construction, but it would ultimately be wrapped in glass. Its developer
couldn't tear down the James T. Brown House, so instead they
left it there and began pouring concrete and erecting steel, higher
and higher, as the shadow cast on the historic home grew longer
and longer. It was Austin's newest and tallest skyscraper, but it
wouldn't be for long; developers had already broken ground on
what would be an even taller building on the other side of town.
Half of the skyscrapers that would dwarf the James T. Brown
House would be residential. The other half had already been
leased by Facebook. It was an almost too-perfect metaphor: a tech
behemoth—the world's largest social media site, no less—literally
enveloping old Austin.

But what was more foreboding was that by November 2022,
Meta, Facebook's parent company, had decided it would no longer
occupy the office space, instead choosing to sublease it, which the
Austin Business Journal said cast a pall over the city's commercial
real estate scene. The new post-pandemic ways of working didn't
call for big fancy offices anymore. Some companies ditched their offices altogether. Remote working, or a hybrid, were de rigueur, and
it looked like this was here to stay. The question then was: Would
Austin's building boom, which showed no signs of slowing, result in
a huge surplus of unwanted office space?

A few blocks north of the James T. Brown House, somewhere
in the bowels of the Austin History Center, there's a single yellowing typewritten sheet of paper, tucked away in a folder. It's a history
of the house, and it says it was built by a school proprietor named
Buford J. Smith after he bought the land at auction from the State
of Texas in 1853. The house Smith built on Sixth and Guadalupe
had an outbuilding that now serves as a garage but, rumor has it,
was once used as slave quarters. The house itself has brick walls
two feet thick, and inside you can still see the marks of hand tools
on much of the woodwork and hand-forged nails, axe marks on the
bricks and oak beams. It has the original wood floors too. The house
is an example of the earliest type of architecture in Austin, and it
has such fine workmanship it was recorded as a Texas historic
landmark in 1968. Two years after Smith built the property, he sold
it to James T. Brown for $400. Brown and his wife, Lucretia, had
three children while they lived there, but their marriage wasn't a
happy one, and Lucretia filed for divorce in 1871, charging her husband with "brutal and outrageous treatment." She got the kids and
the home in the split, and a couple of years later she sold up and
moved on, but twenty years later James Brown won it back at a public auction. In the 1940s, one employee of the Community Chest
(later United Way), which had offices in the house, said she heard
strange noises coming from the basement. They turned out to be
caused by the roots of a tree that had grown next to the retaining
wall. Construction of the Capital National Bank across the street in
the 1950s caused several cracks in the old house, but contractors
said that the blasts necessary to dig the foundations wouldn't cause
any damage. In the 1960s, a subsequent employee noted that they
often wondered what the early occupants of the house would have
thought if they could have seen it then. "The thick rock walls that
had served so well before air conditioning to keep the basement cool
became a sound problem," they wrote. "The noises from key punch,
sorter, reproducer and counting machine bounced back and forth

between those walls. When all the machines were running at the same time I would wear ear phones to deaden the sound."

That yellowing piece of paper I found in the Austin History Center notes that the old house "has survived the years as few modern ones could," but looking at it today, I wondered what the point of survival for old buildings like this was at all if this is what happens to them. I'm from London. Can you imagine my hometown without its old buildings? I can't picture walking out of Tower Hill station and not seeing that imposing chunk of London wall, an ancient Roman fortification built in the second or third century CE to protect the city from invasion, dominating my view to the east. Or Westminster Hall, built in 1097 and from which sprung the major institutions of Britain's government, being razed to make way for a soulless office block. It's unthinkable. We preserve old buildings not just as reminders of a city's past but to help establish the character of a place—some permanence amid rapid cultural change. An old building might be made of materials no longer available, forged by hand with methods long lost to time, or in a style noted for its architectural value. Destroying these old buildings is irreversible.

Today, though, you might agree with me and wonder why it's worth preserving the James T. Brown House at all. The home has lost all context. It's just a sorry-looking single-story building, not in the best condition, now dominated by a nondescript glass, steel, and concrete tower, and in my view it's a sad indictment of the value Austin places on its history.

STAND ON GUADALUPE BETWEEN NINTH and Tenth Streets facing east, and you can see the capitol. Turn your head to the right and you'll see the thirty-six-story-tall Indeed Tower, which was, for a brief moment, the tallest office building downtown. You'll also see what was to be the future home of Meta now dominating the sky, its offices empty. Keep spinning clockwise, and some of old Austin remains: the history center, old-growth oaks, and the beautiful, tiered art deco Travis County Courthouse. Between you and the courthouse is Wooldridge Park, a one-acre space with a white-painted bandstand in the center. This was one of four public squares designated as civic spaces in the original city plan drawn up in 1839 by Edwin Waller, one of Austin's founders. Since it was established, the little park has hosted political rallies, concerts, and gatherings, and since 1983, the view of the Texas state capitol from this park—one of the so-called Capitol View Corridors—has been protected under state and local law from obstruction by tall buildings.

It's here that I met up with Charles Peveto, Candace Volz, and Ted Eubanks. Charles is the architectural historian for the Texas Historical Commission, Candace is a decorative arts historian who sits on the board of the Austin History Center Association, and Ted is a historian with a particular expertise in Austin's past. Ted told me he was concerned that at a time when there are so few homes available to buy in Austin, and none that are reasonably priced, the city is green-lighting office blocks, each one attracting companies bringing ten thousand new jobs, which he likens to "a good-size town." Candace told me it's going to put an incredible stress on the city's already inadequate roadways and infrastructure. "We're sitting at the precipice," Ted said, "and we're going to fall off."

Whenever there's a development proposal that involves a plan to tear down a historic building, it goes before the Historic Landmark Commission, a body that reviews requests to establish or remove historic designations. In the case of the James T. Brown House, there was a compromise. The architect was required to sacrifice a significant portion of the new building's parking garage in order to preserve the historic home. Charles thinks it's all about balance: parity between sensible development and preserving the historical fabric of the city. "I hear comments by some of the developers that they're 'building character,'" he said, pointing to a bland skyscraper in the distance. "The question you have to ask is will we place a preservation order on one of these buildings in fifty years' time?" In most cases, the answer is probably no. Most are uniform, cookie-cutter towers. Nothing about them is unique.

Charles remembers in the late 1980s when the former Texas Medical Association building at Fifteenth and Guadalupe Streets was about to be demolished, and construction workers discovered the original 1840s log cabin inside—the building had literally been built around it, but it had been preserved intact. "It was demolished anyway," he said. "There was no attempt to save it, and by the time our office got wind of it, it was too late."

So what can be done about old buildings currently under threat?

"Prayer helps," Candace said. "That's really all we have."

DOUG MANCHESTER, PRESIDENT OF THE company developing the Fairmont, then Austin's newest downtown hotel, said the city's skyline was shaping up to be "one of the most distinctive," and over the coming decade, he looked forward to seeing "many other unique and iconic towers" that would "elevate Austin as a top 10 most admired metropolitan skyline." I thought back to that photo my friend Kevin Ashton had texted me of Wuhan. Except for the Yellow Crane Tower, a huge pagoda-style structure on the banks of the Yangtze River, the Chinese city's panorama of gray concrete skyscrapers looked, from some angles, just like Austin.

Apart from some interesting buildings—the Frost Bank Tower, the Independent (nicknamed the "Jenga Tower") maybe— Austin's new horizon is bland; what we're witnessing is something that's happening to far too many once interesting and unique places: the homogenization of cities. All across America they're rapidly expanding and, at the same time, increasingly resembling one another. Transformation can be subtle, but the result is just as significant. Cities once hailed as melting pots of diversity and dynamism are being forever changed by gentrification and globalization. Corporate chains. Luxury boutiques. The character and soul of the neighborhood eroded by the relentless march of monoculture. Austin may be prospering, but it's also a sanitized, more boring version of its former self. But why? Why couldn't it—and other cities that have undergone such rapid transformations—retain its unique identity, and at the same time be a vibrant, diverse, and welcoming space for all?

TWO HUNDRED MILES WEST OF Denver, in Colorado's Rocky Mountains, is the luxury ski resort of Aspen. It's a former silver mining town that grew to include churches, banks, schools, even its own opera house, and by the 1930s it had come across the radar of ski enthusiasts. A decade later the Chicago pulp magnate Walter Paepcke and his wife, Elizabeth, saw the commercial potential, but their vision was greater than just a town for ski bums. They founded the Aspen Institute, an internationally renowned ideas festival that brought together scholars and thinkers from across the globe with the lofty ambition of helping address some of the world's most complicated problems. Aspen would go on to host a yearly music festival and design conference; it would get a world-class art museum and see annual theater performances and festivals.

As author Robert Frank wrote in his book *The High-Beta Rich*, Aspen "became a haven for artists, writers, ski bums, and assorted cowboy bohemians who could rail against the establishment but live a comfortable and carefree life in the mountains." Frank noted that the nightlife scene was devoid of velvet ropes and VIP lists. As one oil magnate recalled, "You'd have a society woman next to a ski lift operator next to a construction guy." By most accounts it was a pretty unique place. But by the 1980s, Frank noted, "the quiet old money gave way to proud new money. Entrepreneurs, cable TV magnates, media tycoons, and the first wave of Wall Streeters started pouring in . . . Speaking at a conference in 1987, an aged Elizabeth Paepcke warned of the ill effects of so much new wealth. 'Are we going to kill the golden goose by feeding the animal until its liver becomes distended and we produce a pâté which is so rich that none of us can digest it anymore? What price glory?'" The town Elizabeth had put on the map had changed irreparably, and she declared that her heart was broken.

By the 1990s, Aspen had become one of the richest towns in America, riding the dot-com boom as tech entrepreneurs, real estate moguls, hedge fund bosses, and celebrities moved in, and the irony, much like in Austin, is that the nouveau riche were attracted to Aspen specifically because of its arty, antiestablishment culture. What happened next is a pitch-perfect lesson in gentrification. Unable to afford the exorbitant rents, a lot of the town's small mom-and-pop stores were forced to close, replaced by designer shops. And skiing was superseded as the town's biggest money-maker by the business of real estate sales, each home going under the hammer for increasingly ludicrous amounts. Sound familiar?

Perhaps a more obvious comparison is with San Francisco. In 2014, a series of images of the city by the photographer Scott Hampton, parodying what he saw as the ludicrous situation of its home rental market, went viral. Hampton had stuck "For Rent" signs on mailboxes, trash cans, and planters across the city, taken photos of them, then written up sales pitches for each before posting the results on Craigslist. One example: a dilapidated, graffiti-covered dumpster with an orange "For Rent" sign stuck on the side. "$5000 / 33ft^2 - Waterfront Condo (downtown / civic / van ness): Waterfront condo in the highly desirable, up-and-coming mid-Market area.

CHANGES   163

Enjoy the sounds and smells of the UN Plaza fountain as you relax in your condo after a hard day of complaining about the homeless . . . Utilities not included, nor available." It would be funny if it wasn't so close to the truth, but in 2016, another story went viral of a local man, Peter Berkowitz, who was paying $400 a month to live in what was essentially a wooden box that he'd built in his friend's living room with enough room for a mini bed and folding desk. This, though, wasn't a joke.

San Francisco had undergone one of the most pronounced transformations in the country, experiencing a massive tech boom (in the decade since 2009 the industry grew by 57 percent), building ever-taller skyscrapers and witnessing runaway rents, a worsening homelessness crisis, and an exodus of musicians and artists who could no longer afford to live there. Not for nothing did a movie come out in 2019 with the title *The Last Black Man in San Francisco:* from 1970 to 2010, the city's African American population decreased 50 percent. In his book on San Francisco, *Pictures of a Gone City,* Richard Walker wrote that when well-paid tech workers descended, the absurdly high price of housing resulted in a "tsunami of displacement," forcing millions out of their homes to relocate to the exurbs—people, he said, who worked in the city doing jobs that were neither high-tech nor glamorous. By 2016, housing affordability there had reached a crisis point, with the California Association of Realtors reporting that only 13 percent of city households could afford to purchase the median-priced home. Like Austin, San Francisco seemed oblivious to the environmental impact of all this growth, which would be exacerbated by wildfires, rising sea levels, and other palpable consequences of climate change. The results were, Walker wrote, "what happens when there's untrammeled city building, water consumption, and pollution."

By the dawn of 2015, though, Texas had surpassed California as the country's most overvalued housing market. One Wall Street credit grader reckoned three of the four most overvalued major metro-area housing markets in the United States were in Texas, and of those Austin was the most overvalued, at 20 percent. But real estate markets experience upswings and downswings, booms and busts. They're cyclical. Markets crash. Markets recover. And it's worth noting that by the summer of 2022, for San Francisco at least, one of the most dramatic real estate market upswings in history looked like it had finally peaked. And by peaked I mean the average price of a condo there was now $1.2 million.

I'VE THOUGHT A LOT ABOUT a comment I heard once that Austin is no longer weird and quirky but corporate and pretentious. However, it's still possible to seek out those old Austin haunts to remind yourself what sort of city it used to be. Each time I go back I make a beeline for Cisco's on East Sixth Street, hug Lydia, the waitress who's worked there certainly as long as I've been going, and sit at the round table in the corner on the right of the first of the two back rooms. It's easy, when you're midway through your third cup of black coffee and your belly's full of migas, to look around this room of mismatched furniture and photographs of celebrities and politicians who regularly paid it a visit over the years and forget Austin's changed much at all. When local politician Greg Casar ran (successfully) for Congress in 2022, he said he believed in restaurant unions, affordable housing, Medicare, and breakfasts at Cisco's. Truth is, I don't know how long Cisco's will be around. It's prime real estate, and developers are salivating like hungry wolves. I wouldn't be at all surprised if one day I go back and see a Chili's in its place.

CHAPTER 11

HOMELESS

Gentrification doesn't simply mean investment in an area that results in better services, cleaner roads, prettier city spaces, and more new restaurants than you can possibly visit in a year. That stuff usually comes at a cost: the displacement of long-term, low-income residents and the resegregation of neighborhoods. There's a link between increasing rents and homelessness, and the effect is more pronounced for Black and Hispanic residents.

IN THE LAST CHAPTER, I mentioned the similarities between Austin and San Francisco, including when the California city's home rental market went nuts as a result of its gigantic tech boom. But extortionate rental prices, lack of affordable housing, home prices to make you keel over, and rampant gentrification aren't the only things Austin shares with Fog City. Austin has also found it hard to adequately care for its homeless population. Homelessness certainly existed in San Francisco well before it saw its first tech boom in the 1990s, but there has been little investment in affordable housing, and as the city's tech sector grew, so did evictions. Landlords kicked out existing tenants so they could lease to people prepared to pay much more for the same places, while elsewhere investors tore down rent-controlled buildings, replacing them with posh apartments. When I first moved to Austin, the city had just come tenth on a list published by the National Coalition for the Homeless of the twenty "meanest cities" in America for homeless people. Back then Austin legislators were considering a ban on street sleeping and curbside begging. You'd see homeless people panhandling from the medians the length and breadth of the city and at stoplights on the I-35 service road downtown, sleeping under overpasses, and begging outside bars on Sixth Street.

A month or so after my friend Luke and I left Austin to continue on our road trip across America back in 1999, we'd arrived in San Francisco, and I remember thinking the homelessness problem there was tragically bad. We stayed in a youth hostel in the SoMa neighborhood, and on the streets outside, homeless people were everywhere, pushing grocery carts full of blankets, jackets, and their meager belongings along sidewalks. Austin was a much smaller city, but it seemed to have an outsized homelessness problem too.

BACK IN THE LATE 1980S, when Austin's economy began to tank—its tech industry hit hard by the recession, leading to layoffs and decreased investment—the city's homeless population increased in line with lost jobs and evictions. Up to two hundred people a night slept on mats on the concrete floors of homeless shelters with rats and cockroaches; others camped out in public parks or in their cars. There were some improvements in the early 1990s, as the city enacted some policies aimed at preserving and expanding affordable housing, but by the end of the decade the city council had adopted a "no camping" ordinance. If a homeless person violated the ban, he or she could get fined $500, land themselves with a Class C misdemeanor, and face being arrested if he or she didn't show up to court.

Over the years there have been numerous plans, assessment reports, and task forces assembled to try to address homelessness in Austin, but the problem just seems to get worse. In the 2000s, the city's population was growing faster than new housing could be built, and any efforts to create affordable housing were often met with opposition from residents concerned about their property values and neighborhood character. In 2004, the Austin Resource Center for the Homeless (ARCH) opened, providing shelter, food, and health care to the city's unhoused, but it was never going to be a cure-all. Amber Fogarty, who then chaired the committee of a group of nonprofits pushing for more resources for the homeless, told me in her view Texas had a shameful record of dealing with social issues; of the annual $11 million set aside for funding Austin's homeless services in 2010, 62 percent came from the city, 27 percent from the federal government, and just 11 percent from the state.

BACK THEN, IN 2010, I visited a homeless camp behind a business off South Lamar Boulevard. It was close to a road, near shops and offices in a busy stretch of Austin, but you'd never know it was there, that people slept and ate and passed their days and nights here in obscurity. One of the men living there was William Clay, a forty-seven-year-old South Carolinian who had a broad, gap-toothed smile, despite suffering from a blood disease and cirrhosis of the liver. Clay was a military vet and told me he'd been hospitalized fourteen times in the past three years for his health issues. He worked an occasional construction shift to earn cash, and when he did it meant he was able to eat at McDonald's or Taco Bell that day.

I met another of Austin's homeless residents in Zilker Park. Todd Dean, fifty-one, who sported a ponytail and baseball cap, had been sleeping in his car for a year. In the early 1980s, he'd earned a business degree at the University of Texas and worked in corporate America until a girlfriend introduced him to drugs. He got addicted, lost his job, fell behind on mortgage payments, had his condo foreclosed on, and ended up on the sidewalk. Some of Todd's friends blamed his girlfriend, but he didn't. "I'm not a lamb being led to the slaughter," he told me. "The addiction crept up on me." Destitute and living on the streets of Austin, he said it was a fight for survival. "There's a lot of violence and death out there. There are people you meet one day, and the next, you're reading about them in the obituary column. When I'm in my car, I'm basically exposing myself to whoever might happen by. I usually lock my doors and keep my windows barely cracked, but that danger is real and does exist."

AT THE TIME, THE CITY estimated there were about a thousand "chronically homeless" people in Austin. Today that figure is more like 2,300. And around one in every three people in Austin's homeless population is Black—a troubling statistic when you consider that Black people account for around one in ten Austinites. Almost 60 percent of homeless people in Austin are men, and the majority of the city's homeless (35.2 percent) are between the ages of twenty-five and forty-four. In 2022, when rents soared to three times the national average, it's unsurprising that people became houseless quicker than Austin could find a place to put them. This isn't that difficult a concept to grasp: when housing supply can't keep up with demand, prices go up, and this increases the chances that people who are already living paycheck to paycheck will be driven out of their homes. A report in 2021 titled "A Rising Tide Drowns Unstable Boats: How Inequality Creates Homelessness" showed that in a community of 740,000 people where income disparities had risen sharply over a decade, it could expect more than 550 additional people experiencing homelessness on any given night.

Austin's treatment of homelessness as an issue hasn't necessarily been dramatically worse than similar cities its size. But
some places, like Columbus, Ohio, have proactively implemented
an approach known as Housing First, where providing permanent housing to people experiencing homelessness is prioritized
with no caveats. Houseless people don't have to address behav-
ioral health problems or agree to participate in certain services
in order to "qualify." Housing First means unconditional access to
housing, and as a result, in 2018 that city saw a 70 percent success
rate for housing its homeless population.

Austin's got some way to go to catch up. If you were wondering if there was an anecdote that perfectly encapsulated the chasm
between the tech wealth that was coming to Austin, which a lot
of this book is about, and the city's most vulnerable individuals,
in 2012 the SXSW festival delivered. On the sidewalk outside the
convention center stood Clarence, a middle-aged homeless African
American man who lost everything in Hurricane Katrina before
coming to Austin. Clarence wore a black beanie and a white T-shirt
that read: "I'm Clarence, a 4G Hotspot." He was one of thirteen men
that the British (apologies) advertising firm Bartle Bogle Hegarty
had asked to roam the streets of Austin offering wireless access via
loaner hotspots in return for a donation, which Clarence and his
fellow "hotspots" could keep. But the "Homeless Hotspots" marketing campaign didn't quite get the sort of press that perhaps Bartle
Bogle Hegarty hoped it might. *Wired* magazine said it sounded
"like something out of a darkly satirical science-fiction dystopia,"
while one tech blogger said that "the digital divide has never hit us
over the head with a more blunt display of unselfconscious gall." I
struggle to think of a more tone-deaf publicity stunt.

BACK IN 2010, ALAN GRAHAM was a regular sight around Austin in his white pickup truck. He was in his early fifties, and the

day I first met him he wore a ball cap and had a full white beard. He had moved to Austin from Houston decades before to go to college but had dropped out of UT and ended up working in real estate for twenty-five years. By the time we met he'd spent more than a decade running a homeless charity called Mobile Loaves & Fishes, checking in on his "clients," as he called them, around the city and helping distribute food and slowly building his operation. Part of MLF's mission was to house Austin's homeless in gently used recreational vehicles so they could take pride in having their own space and in being part of a community. To Alan, that was crucial, and he had some big plans for the future. At the time, MLF was trying to buy a piece of land out by the airport, not far from where my new house was. Alan envisaged a community in which residents had access to counseling and people who could help them find work. I wouldn't see Alan again for twelve years, and in that time the homelessness situation in Austin had gotten worse as the city grew. Meanwhile, Alan had been working tirelessly in the wings, refusing to give up his dream of doing his not-insignificant bit to help Austin's homeless.

I MET UP WITH HIM again in the spring of 2022. In the intervening years he had built a fifty-one-acre community of affordable, permanent housing, and he wanted to give me a tour. The sun was shining the morning I arrived at the Community First! Village, about seven miles east of downtown, and there were agaves and cacti planted in a rocky garden near the entrance. Alan hadn't changed much since I last saw him—he still sported that neat white beard and a baseball cap (this one read "Goodness"), and today he wore black-rimmed glasses, a Columbia fishing shirt, and a crucifix around his neck. He told me MLF had bought another fifty-one acres across the street and was about to break ground on that, and it also owned a seventy-six-acre plot some fifteen minutes away. At that time 320 people lived at the village; in eight years' time Alan reckoned two thousand people would call this place home. They were responsible for paying rent and for their own meals. A 399-square-foot rental home or RV started at $430 a month, plus electricity and propane. In a remarkable example of "walking the walk," Alan lived there too, in a mobile home with a screened-in porch and an extensive collection of yard art that included a rustic wagon wheel, Coke sign, and terra-cotta Virgin Mary. The porch, he told me, "is where we panhandle the millionaires and billionaires." He later added that he wasn't joking about having billionaires on his porch whom he would tap for donations.

We spent an hour touring the community in Alan's golf cart. Each mobile home was yellow, gray, or teal, and residents had added their own flourishes like hanging baskets or yard art. Alan has a somewhat unique take on Austin's lack of affordable housing in that he believes the problem is not affordability at all; it's transportation. "We're surrounded by land everywhere, and we could easily build affordable housing communities where people could buy a house for $100,000 or $150,000 and live out the American dream," he said. So why don't we? "Because we're a fucked-up, elitist group of people who say, 'Not in my backyard.' That's why I think transportation's the only way out of this. If you want some-body to clean your toilet in your house every day, and you only want to pay him fifteen or twenty bucks an hour, he's got to live somewhere. So either pay him fifty bucks an hour or we need to figure out transportation."

He's right on the housing part, of course, but I don't believe trans-portation is the magic bullet. It's only part of the solution. Pushing the less well-off to the suburbs first, then the exurbs, then farther out to towns miles and miles away, isn't the answer. It's shortsighted because property values and taxes will only get greater out there too. And then what? Keep extending the rail line and bus routes until cleaners and line cooks have to commute to Austin from Midland?

In Alan's office, a huge coffee table book called *The Amazing Faith of Texas* sat on a stand on the windowsill and, next to that, the paperback edition of Alan's memoir, *Welcome Homeless*. His Labrador Frannie sat in a kennel in front of his desk. Doing what Alan does in Austin involves a balancing act, because he's working in a liberal city in a red state and often has to seek help from politicians of both stripes, going cap in hand to raise money from Democrats and Republicans alike.

"Periodically I like watching MMA fighting," he told me. "I like to see men and women get into the octagon and beat the living fuck out of each other . . . then oftentimes, when the deal's over, they're hugging it out and congratulating each other." It's a metaphor I wasn't quite expecting. Alan explained, "I just got off of the phone with a buddy of mine who's running for Congress and wanted our support. But I don't give political support because I don't want to be in the octagon."

Alan understands politics. When Greg Abbott signed a bill in 2021 banning homeless encampments on public property, Alan shrugged. Politics. He's more concerned that for a city that likes to wave the "progressive" flag, Austin is hypocritical when it comes to the homeless. He thinks it's an "extraordinarily elitist" place, despite being a city he loves more than any other on the planet. I recalled that when I met Alan more than a decade earlier and he told me about his dream of housing the homeless in places of their own rather than in shelters, some plots of land he'd identified didn't work out because neighbors objected to homeless people being housed there. NIMBYism was alive and well in Austin—especially, as far as Alan was concerned, among its apparently progressive residents.

Alan is nothing if not optimistic, though. He truly believes that transportation is key to Austin's affordability problem—so that, as he told me, you could buy cheap property in nearby cities like La Grange, Burnet, San Marcos, and New Braunfels and establish a decent rail system to take people to and from those places. He dreams of high-speed, elevated trains traveling at 120 miles an hour that can transport you from these new commuter towns to downtown Austin in thirty minutes, of autonomous vehicles so there are no more traffic accidents. "We have to think outside the box," he said. The problem is that those cities and towns he mentioned are no longer affordable either. Prices have gone up. And there's no transportation fix in the short term. It's sick that a city as wealthy and apparently progressive as Austin has a homelessness problem so pronounced. But it's there for all to see: a dissonance between the values the city's known for (and which it loves to parade) and what it's become.

There are few more compelling examples of this than Leslie Cochran. An Austin fixture for decades, this homeless cross-dresser embodied the "Keep Austin Weird" schtick the city so loves to champion. But here's the irony: Leslie was the perfect, palatable show pony; the pinnacle of Austin eccentricity, but one which the city and the media could stomach. On camera, he was charming, lovable. The fact that he spent his short life railing against injustice and attempting to achieve civil rights for the homeless was neither here nor there. That wasn't the story—he was. Meanwhile, in the years since his death in 2012 at the age of sixty (his health problems had worsened in the few years since he suffered a head injury, suspected to have been caused by a fall following a stroke), violence against homeless folks in Austin has only increased. And the lack of real investment in affordable housing, housing for the homeless, and mental health services continues.

TIM SHEA MOVED INTO ALAN'S Community First! Village in 2018. Three years later, Alan offered him the chance to occupy a brand-new home on the property, and the day he did, Tim also found himself in the unusual position of being the first person in the United States to live in a 3D-printed house. It's incredible to watch the process: a gigantic silver arm delivers a smooth, perfectly formed bead of concrete like toothpaste from a tube, following the architectural specifications laid out for the walls of the house. It takes forty-eight hours to "print" those walls. The result is a smart, urban cabin that apparently costs around 20 to 30 percent less than a tiny home would using traditional construction methods. There are several of these now at Community First! Village.

Tim was born in Connecticut in 1951 into a family that he said had a predisposition for addiction. He ended up in reform school, and by the time he was done it was 1968 and the middle of the counterculture. Tim threw himself headfirst into the drug and rock and roll lifestyle, reading Ginsberg and Ferlinghetti, hitchhiking back and forth across America, having a wild time. Tim was a hippie with no ties, and if he ever ran into any heavy situation—romantic, financial—he'd just stick his head in the sand and disappear. Unlike most of his friends, though, Tim never left the party, and in the mid-1970s, after getting caught selling heroin, he ended up in the Ohio State Penitentiary. While he was inside, he edited the prison newspaper; writing was something that came naturally to Tim, and after his sentence was reduced and he was released in 1976, he got accepted into the journalism program at Ohio State University. For a time, he worked for a bureau of the *Cleveland Plain Dealer* newspaper, but then he relapsed. "This is always the last sentence of each story I tell," he told me: "I went back on the street, and I went back to prison."

He had a brother who lived in Grand Prairie, near Dallas, so when he got out, Tim headed to Texas. He worked at a bookstore, met a girl, spent weekends on a ranch with her friends near Austin, and fell in love with the city. Then someone got shot at a dope house in Dallas while Tim was there, and although he wasn't the shooter and the victim didn't die, Tim was sentenced to thirty years under the state's "law of parties," a notorious and controversial piece of Texas legislation that says you can be criminally liable for the actions of another under certain circumstances. This time, while he was back in prison, Tim was offered the chance to take part in an in-house drug program, the first of its kind, which was supported by then governor Ann Richards. He was sent to a five-hundred-bed treatment center in Kyle, south of Austin, and told if he completed the course he'd see his sentence cut drastically. Tim was released in 1993 and sent to work in Austin, where he said the city embraced him. He was even invited to the governor's mansion to meet Ann Richards in person. After another relapse, though, which violated the terms of his parole, he was back in prison again, this time for seven years. He finally got out in 2004, and Tim has lived in Austin ever since. He still used drugs—not as much, but it was still just as destructive. He also had chronic arthritis and struggled to walk. He had regular spells of homelessness too. The longest was when he lived behind a retention wall next to a business on South Congress. After a while he introduced himself to the woman who owned the business, and she and her husband invited him to stay near the entrance to their ranch off William Cannon Drive instead. It was safer there, and they brought Tim a fan and dragged an extension cord down from the house so he'd have electricity. Eventually they even bought him a small travel trailer and set it up on the same spot so he could live there temporarily.

One day Tim heard about Alan Graham and Mobile Loaves & Fishes. The Community First! Village project was still in its infancy, and Alan suggested Tim might be a good candidate to get his own place. He was one of the first people to move in, and today, while he knows a relapse is possible, in the few years he's lived there he's forged so many bonds with other tenants and staff—not to mention Alan—that he's fearful of disappointing them if he does.

TIM FELL FOR AUSTIN A long time ago—in between relapses, in the middle of one of his many stories that always, inevitably, ended with him back on the street and then back in a prison cell. Like a lot of people, it seems, he ended up in Austin by a twist of fate. The city had offered him the chance to reinvent himself, to start again. Tim had experienced that sliding-doors moment I had and that Brian Case, the young man who had taken his life the day I first arrived, had.

AUSTIN'S HOMELESS POPULATION HAS BECOME a political football in a tussle between the state, the city council, and the public in what to do with them. For more than twenty years, the police simply moved them (or forced them to move) to places that were less visible to the public like tent encampments, hidden in the city's green spaces. Then, in 2019, the city council voted to soften its policy banning camping in public, loitering in certain areas, and panhandling. Governor Greg Abbott called it reckless and insane, and two years on Austinites voted to reinstate the ban. Police began by clearing out dozens of people living in the most visible encampment, a stone's throw from police headquarters underneath the I-35 underpass downtown. Since then they've continued to try to enforce the ban, but with few shelters for homeless folks to actually move to, the problem has become intractable. Homelessness in Austin increased by more than a hundred percent between 2022 and 2023. The city is building more housing for them; it's already converted two former hotels into hostels and has pledged to build a thousand more homes for them by 2024. But it feels so belated, and meanwhile homeless people are still being shuffled from place to place, out of sight and out of mind of Austin's expanding population.

I REMEMBER SOMETHING TODD DEAN told me when we chatted in Zilker Park back in 2010 when he was living in his car. He'd said there was a lot of violence and death on the streets in Austin, that he would lock his car doors at night when he was sleeping because "the danger [was] real." It chimed with something Austin's former police chief told me a few years later. Art Acevedo said that people didn't appreciate Austin was no longer a small town, that it was now a "big city, with big-city problems." In 2012, in the early hours one morning at the end of July, a forty-nine-year-old homeless man named William Greer wandered to a quiet stretch of the hike-and-bike trail downtown, a few feet from Lady Bird Lake, climbed into his sleeping bag, and fell asleep. At eight the next morning, someone walking their dog found Greer's lifeless body: he'd been bludgeoned to death. Detectives investigating a murder usually begin by talking to people the victim knew: friends, family, colleagues. But Greer didn't have a partner or a job and hadn't spoken to anyone in his family for months. Police ruled out robbery as a motive: he still had cash and credit cards on him. The killing seemed to be motiveless, there were no suspects, and detectives had no leads. His death bore similarities to that of another homeless man in Austin eight months earlier; like Greer, David Max Tucker was bludgeoned to death at night, his body found the next morning on East Riverside Drive. At the time, Austin police solved about 90 percent of murder cases. In 2012, Greer's murder was one of only two that they failed to solve.

There's a term, "less dead," that refers to how some murder victims—prostitutes, the poor, migrant farm workers, runaways, the homeless—are largely ignored by the wider community they live in and generally not missed by society if they disappear or die. I was drawn to reporting Greer's story because, for me, it spoke volumes about the place I felt Austin was becoming.

The year I arrived, there were 4 murders per 100,000 people. By 2021, there were 8.2—more per capita than Boston, San Diego, or Seattle; that year Austin counted 89 homicides, a record since police began keeping a tally in the 1960s. The crime rate was rising faster than Austin's population was growing. Meanwhile, back in London, where I'd come from, the murder rate in 2021 was 1.5 per 100,000 people. I had to wonder if Austin was simply the best option for many people with fewer options.

Today, Austin's destitute seek shelter in the shadow of its new skyscrapers, and as the city's population swells, so too does their number. On one single day in January 2022, of the 3,247 people identified as being homeless in Austin, 2,374 of them were un-sheltered, meaning they were sleeping in tents, cars, or abandoned buildings or on the roadside. By the summer of 2023, there were 5,455. Austin's homeless have been forced to move farther and farther from downtown to ever more secluded areas, pushed to the margins of this big city with big-city problems.

CHAPTER 12

GROWING PAINS

Austin's airport does a very good job perpetuating the "Live Music Capital" sobriquet. In fact, Austin's airport does a very good job convincing you that you don't actually need to leave the airport at all to experience Austin. Once you're through security, there are the predictable stores selling rhinestone-embellished tops, cowboy boots, and "Keep Austin Weird" T-shirts. But there are also a lot of the very same restaurants and coffee shops you'll find across the city if you did happen to leave the confines of the airport: Austin institutions like Ruta Maya, ThunderCloud Subs, Tacodeli, the Salt Lick BBQ, Second Bar + Kitchen, and East Side Pies. There are stages too, where you can watch Austin bands like Asleep at the Wheel ply their trade. It's nice to see independent shops and food outlets rather than the national chains you usually see at other airports, and it's a great touch showcasing local bands, but something about it feels odd—like Austin itself has been commodified, watered down and packaged. It reminds me of what Will Sheff of the band Okkervil River told me: that he thought people had begun to bottle the spirit of Austin and market it.

In fact, in 2019, airport officials had the bright idea that Austinites might love their airport so much that they would want to go through security just to spend time there, even if they had no plans to actually fly anywhere. Imagine: it's Saturday and you're wondering what to do for the evening. And rather than go to a club downtown, which in all likelihood is probably going to shut down soon anyway because its owners can't afford the exorbitant rent, you make the actual conscious decision to drive instead to Austin's gleaming airport, park in the short stay, flash your passport for the TSA agent, and then watch a band on a sterile, polished stage while munching on barbecue from the Salt Lick. *Come to the Live Music Capital of the World. It was always a publicity stunt anyway.*

Just contemplating this scenario makes me miss the old Emo's on Sixth and Red River Streets and that unmistakable smell of beer and sweat and bleach, whose urinals may have been clogged with gum but whose walls were a living, breathing art museum. It makes me pine for the old days—days that really aren't that old at all in the grand scheme of things—of quiet, sunbaked streets; of cheap Tex-Mex, hole-in-the-wall bars, and twenty-four-hour cafés playing obscure records on repeat. Forgive me while I wax nostalgic for a bit, but that's the way of Austin: you never quite believe that the good parts could go away.

Near gate 14 in the airport, there's a restaurant called Hut's Hamburgers, and I think the fact it's there just might be the most telling illustration of what's happening outside those thick brick walls. Hut's original location on South Congress opened in 1939 before it moved to West Sixth Street in the late 1960s. It served up the usual fries, onion rings, and shakes, and its beef patties were regularly voted best burger in town. In 2019, though, after eighty years, Hut's shut its downtown doors for good. Today the airport location is all that's left—a castrated version of itself. The burgers may taste the same, but there's more to a restaurant than just the food. Gone is the red-and-black-checkered linoleum flooring, the neon beer signs, the too-close-together diner tables, the mounted bison head, the football pennants draped from the ceiling, the waitresses who called you "sug" and "hon," and the framed black-and-white photos on the wall that documented eight decades serving Austin.

HUT'S WASN'T THE ONLY AUSTIN staple shutting down because of economic pressure. A year earlier Hill's Café on South Congress, which first opened in 1947 and served its customers chicken-fried steak and live music, closed to make way for six hundred apartments, retail and office space, and a hotel. The Goodnight family that founded the café still have a financial interest in the land, and there's a rumor that Hill's may one day make a comeback—a nod to Austin's past embedded in a swanky new development, perhaps.

Austin lost another institution in 2018 when Threadgill's World Headquarters on Riverside Drive closed. Its owner, Eddie Wilson, said, "Property taxes have just gone through the roof . . . We do $4 million a year in gross business, but we don't make anything, because the property taxes increased 350 to 450 percent in the last five years." Fear not, read the reports of its demise, Threadgill's original location on North Lamar, which opened in 1933, was not going anywhere. Kenneth Threadgill, who had been a bootlegger during Prohibition, had bought what was previously a Gulf filling station and, armed with Travis County's first post-Prohibition beer license, turned it into a bar and music venue. Back in those days, Threadgill's friends would play guitar and fiddle in return for free beer, but by the mid-1960s, a young Janis Joplin, who was studying art at UT, had become the venue's star attraction, and Threadgill, her mentor. Threadgill closed the bar in 1974 after his wife died, and it lay empty for several years. In 1979, a fire almost destroyed the building, but Eddie Wilson, who founded the legendary Armadillo World Headquarters, bought, rebuilt, and reopened it in 1981. Kenneth Threadgill lived just long enough to see his bar reborn. In 2018, Wilson hoped the remaining restaurant might become a magnet for people looking to get back in touch with the good old days. But two years later, in the midst of the coronavirus pandemic, Wilson was forced to close the original location too, and after eighty-seven years that magnet attracting people to a taste of Austin's past was gone forever.

CHANGE WAS HAPPENING SO RAPIDLY you could hardly catch a breath. In the summer of 2018, a deal was brokered that would see Austin get its first ever major league sports team, another rung on the ladder to becoming a much larger and very different town. The City of Austin had joined forces with a developer to build a new stadium in northwest Austin in order to bring Major League Soccer to the city. The nearest NBA team was the Spurs in San Antonio; the nearest NFL and MLB teams were 165 miles away in Houston. Anthony Precourt, the owner of the MLS team in Columbus, Ohio, had announced the previous year that he was exploring a move to Austin. Not only that, but actor Matthew McConaughey wanted a minority stake. There was star power behind the bid, and a year later Precourt announced a $45 million deal with St. David's HealthCare to partner on a training and medical care facility for Austin FC's athletes.

It wasn't all plain sailing, though. Precourt's preferred plot was a swath of parkland called Butler Shores next to Auditorium Shores on the banks of Lady Bird Lake, but concerned members of the community thwarted that plan. The same thing happened when Precourt and his consortium wanted to build the stadium at Roy G. Guerrero Colorado River Metropolitan Park, just to the west of Ed Bluestein Boulevard, not far from where we lived. This time opposition grew to public protests and rallies. "Hands Off Guerrero," read one sign. "No Corporate Soccer Stadium on Austin's Public Parkland," read another.

Precourt hired a real estate attorney, Richard Suttle, to smooth the passage of securing a stadium site. Suttle was adamant that this adolescent city was turning into a big city, "and a big city needs a sports team," but in the end, Precourt had to settle for a site twenty minutes north of downtown near the intersection of Burnet Road and Braker Lane. The president of the company operating Austin FC was Dave Greeley, who had been the chief marketing officer of the Chicago Bears football team. Greeley said that they were advised early on that part of getting the deal done in Austin was that they needed to understand that Austin was the coolest kid in town. "Austin is an amazing city," he said, "but it's also kind of an arrogant city. They don't need you. They don't care about you . . . We wanted the people of Austin to want us, but recognized that they didn't need us." Despite protesters rallying against the developers' first choices for the stadium site; despite Austin's mayor, Steve Adler, claiming the city never felt like it needed an MLS team in order "to prove itself"; despite the fact Austin made it seem like it was doing Precourt and his Major League Soccer ambitions a favor by allowing them to come there in the first place, Austin got its first ever major league sports team, and Austin FC's first home game was on June 19, 2021, against the San Jose Earthquakes.

IN THE FALL OF 2018, Austin was about to see the wettest September in the state's history—what some were calling an "aquapocalypse." Seven years earlier, it had seen ninety days over 100 degrees Fahrenheit in a single year, not to mention the hottest day since it began keeping records. Austin was in the grip of a drought-and-flood cycle that was the inevitable consequence of a changing climate. Greg Meszaros, who at the time was the director of Austin Water, said flooding in the Highland Lakes had sent the equivalent of four and a half Niagara Falls downstream per second. Along the railing overlooking the stretch of Lady Bird Lake opposite city hall, there are plaques commemorating the historic floods of the 1900s that overwhelmed the city. This time, it was communities upriver in the Highland Lakes region that would endure the worst damage: seven feet of water filling up houses; floodwaters destroying playground equipment in parks, ripping up blacktop and trees, washing bridges away. At one point it threatened to flood downtown Austin. Instead, the deluge of rainwater caused such huge levels of silt buildup and mud that Austin's water treatment facility struggled to cope with the extra filtration that was needed. For the first time in the city's history, officials issued a "boil water" notice. "Immediate action is needed to avoid running out of water," Austin Water told customers. It was an emergency that would impact hospitals, schools, universities, and food services—"simply a case of Mother Nature throwing more at the system than the system can currently process," city manager Spencer Cronk said. Customers were told to use hand sanitizer after they washed their hands; stores limited patrons to four multipacks of bottled water—and that's when they hadn't run out altogether.

This was the way weather in Austin would be from now on. Unpredictable. Sometimes devastating. But more drought and heat and fire and flooding would be met, perhaps predictably, by a governor who had zero effective policies to tackle them, in a state that had the highest greenhouse gas emissions in the country by some margin. In August 2017, I'd made a nighttime drive to Houston—through a thunderstorm and two tornado warnings, on a highway only part of which I could make out unfurling in front of me—in order to report on Hurricane Harvey. The category 4 storm had made landfall on the Texas coast and was the largest to hit the state since 1961. On the outskirts of the city I saw an abandoned car, almost entirely submerged, its passenger door wide open beneath the waterline. I saw residential streets entirely cut off by floodwater, an underpass full up to the bridge above with water. Fifteen trillion gallons of rain was deluging America's fourth-largest city. And Greg Abbott simply said disasters like this were "really rather timeless." When a journalist pressed him on the relationship between hurricanes like Harvey and climate change, he replied, "I'm not a scientist, and it's impossible for me to answer that."

I'm no scientist either, but in my almost twenty years living there, I saw firsthand how the climate was changing Texas.

There were other consequences of a changing climate on life in Austin. For years the city has ranked as one of the worst in the country for allergy sufferers, but scientists say it's only going to get worse. While I was on the campus of St. Edward's University talking to climate experts, I met their colleague Roy Johnson, the campus arborist. Austin's been seeing a longer growing season, he told me, and, with that, pests and diseases from other parts of the country—possibly the world—that wouldn't have been able to survive here before. With a longer growing period, the city's also witnessing a longer-lasting allergy season. "Because it's warmer for longer, plants aren't slowing down, and they haven't been doing that for a few years. This has allowed pollen counts to build up and insects and diseases to move in, and our plants don't have defenses against them," Roy told me. He also said it upsets what's known as "phenology"—when you can expect an ecosystem to do certain things at a particular time of year. In the past you could set a date and know that within a week or two certain plants would flower and then insects would arrive to pollinate them. But now it's out of whack. Plants are flowering way before they're supposed to, and insects may be migrating somewhere else because of it.

Predictably, belief in what's happening—and what to do about it—is sharply divided along party lines. A survey of Texas voters in 2019, two years after Hurricane Harvey struck, showed 88 percent of Democrats believed climate change was happening and 79 percent thought the government should be doing a substantial amount to address it. This contrasted with 44 percent of Republicans polled who thought climate change was happening and 18 percent who said the government should be doing "a great deal" or "a lot" to combat it.

Just as when Jim Inhofe, the Republican senator from Oklahoma, brought a snowball onto the floor of the Senate in order to mock those who believed in global warming, the Texas floods of 2018 fueled the fire of the state's climate deniers. But rain falling all at once like it did in 2018 can be devastating. It runs off into drainage channels and streams rather than soaking into the ground because parched soil is less likely to absorb water, and this does little to alleviate the impact of drought. Water that soaks regularly, over several months, into the soil recharges groundwater and sustains trees and vegetation. Catastrophic floods don't. And now worsening floods are just another climate-related problem Texas has to deal with.

By the dawn of 2019, Texas was now leading the nation in two horrifying metrics: heat-related work deaths and infant and toddlers dying in hot cars. Scientific research organization Climate Central reckoned Texas faces the "most extreme heat danger" in the United States, and yet, it said, the state was failing when it came to actually addressing its heat risks. And the report found that the number of potentially dangerous days is rising throughout the country, but particularly in the Southeast—and in Texas specifically.

WHILE THE PRIMARY WORRY FOR Shannon and me had been guns, by this point, the changes in our beloved city were so profound that we'd all but packed our bags and left. Much as it pained us, the quality of life those early, hazy days of Austin promised—hiking, having casual drinks, attending concerts—it felt like a different lifetime. A different place. The traffic was getting worse, if that was possible, and we were forced to use cars because there was no decent public transport. It felt like we weren't getting a spring or fall anymore, just stiflingly hot summers that lasted from April till November.

But ignoring the terrifying reality of climate change just for a moment, Austin had just been bestowed the honor of being the 2018 "Best Place to Live" in America. The accolade was conferred on the city by *U.S. News & World Report,* which based its rankings on affordability, job prospects, and quality of life. High-tech jobs now accounted for almost 16 percent of jobs in the city, and that sector grew by 6.6 percent in 2018. The average annual salary in Austin across the board was a little over $62,000; the average salary for a tech worker, just shy of $119,000. "When deciding on a place to settle down," the publication's executive editor said, "it's important to understand that where a person lives can impact their well-being . . . The top-ranked places are areas where citizens can feel the most fulfilled socially, physically, and financially."

At this point, the only thing about Austin I found fulfilling was my friends. Shannon and I had established lifelong relationships with people we loved, and we'd often moan along with them about the unbearable heat and the palpable changes taking place in the city we all called home. It's easy to turn it around and say *we* had changed, not Austin; that the things I was looking for when I joined Shannon there weren't the same now that we were parents. But both were true: Austin's changes were measurable, and over the years I'd been there it just wasn't the same city I'd fallen in love with all that time ago.

One evening over beers, some friends who lived nearby showed us images of picturesque cabins in Montana and Wyoming they'd been eyeing on Zillow; they'd also thought seriously about leaving and making a new life in the mountains, but both their sets of parents lived just outside Austin, their kids were settled in school, and it seemed too hard for them to just up and go. In some respects we felt lucky we didn't have any parental ties to Austin itself. Shannon's lived in Dallas, and we didn't want to move there. In fact, those first conversations we had with friends about where we were anticipating moving—to the Northeast where we could experience seasons again, where we would be thirty minutes from the mountains and less than two hours from the ocean— were exciting. But as the reality of our decision to leave set in and as our likely departure date got closer, those conversations got progressively harder. In the end, we knew we'd have to leave Austin and the community we'd built and loved behind.

We'd decided, eventually, on New York State. When I told one of the climate scientists at St. Edward's this at the end of our conversation about how global warming was impacting Austin, he'd told me that in terms of climate change, the Hudson Valley was a remarkably good choice. It enjoys a moderate climate with relatively mild summers and winters (it gets snow but nowhere near as much as places in northern New York like Buffalo), and it's far less susceptible to extreme weather like hurricanes, tornadoes, and wildfires. We wanted to live somewhere that was a shorter flight back to London to see my parents too. What's more, we'd done our research into which states were statistically safer when it came to gun violence: New York was the fourth safest in the country, in terms of gun deaths when adjusted for population, after Massachusetts, Hawaii, and New Jersey. We had no expectations that our next home would be perfect. Nowhere is. And we knew it may not be forever too. But we felt ready to move away. We just weren't sure exactly when.

MUCH AS WE HOPED FOR changes to gun laws and better control, it wasn't happening. We weren't feeling safer. And in the summer of 2019, something happened that would force our hand; something that told us if there was ever any doubt in our mind about moving, that doubt was now gone.

It was already just shy of 100 degrees at lunchtime when a student journalist sitting in her car next to Pease Park, less than a mile from the Texas state capitol, dialed 911 to report that a young white man wearing a plaid shirt had removed several guns from the trunk of his vehicle and was now walking toward a large group of children and their families laughing and playing on the park's splash pad. Pease Park is a half mile from Pease Elementary School, the oldest in Texas; both are named after Elisha Pease, a Texas governor in the 1800s. The park is Austin's oldest, and after the school bell rang and on weekends and holidays, kids and their parents would come here to use the splash pad, jungle gym, or picnic tables. Olive, then eight years old, was a third-grade student at Pease. "I don't want to scare anybody," the student told the dispatcher, her voice shaking. "He has an assault rifle and this is not a hunting area." When the families at the splash pad spotted him, they ran.

We were in England, visiting my parents, when Shannon tilted her laptop toward me; we stared at the home page of the *Austin American-Statesman* website in disbelief. Before I moved to America, every time an actual mass shooting made the news, I was just another Brit gawking in horror at a crazy American phenomenon that felt so alien to us. This latest incident was far too close for comfort. It was in our backyard. In a place we trusted with our child.

When police arrived, they found a twenty-three-year-old man they later identified as Dalton Broesche with a knife strapped to his belt and a 9mm pistol in his waistband. Broesche told officers he'd hidden an assault rifle and a thirty-round magazine behind some nearby trees. "I made a huge mistake," he told them. "My life is ruined." Inside his car they found the receipt for a gun he'd recently bought, and a background check flagged an outstanding arrest warrant for assaulting a family member with a weapon. But Texas law said you could buy a gun even if there was a warrant out for your arrest—as long as you hadn't fled the state. So police charged Broesche with two misdemeanors. This was Texas, and he hadn't strictly *done* much of anything.

Perhaps realizing the optics, prosecutors quietly dropped the misdemeanor charges, replacing them with a felony charge of "tampering with physical evidence"—namely hiding his weapons when police approached. Broesche's case labored its way through the court system, going through adjournment after adjournment, warranting barely a mention in the papers. Eventually, he'd serve around five months in jail before returning to live with his parents outside of Austin as a free man, his life very much *not* ruined. But Broesche's face—that mop of mousy hair; his thin, angular chin and wispy goatee; and those staring black eyes—was etched in my brain. I couldn't stop wondering what he planned to do that day. What if Olive had been playing on the splash pad on August 14? What if that student journalist hadn't seen him? What if . . . ? The incident served as a catalyst for our move away from Austin and Texas, but the truth is those feelings had been percolating for years. Our yearlong stay in England between 2014 and 2015 was, it transpired, a sign that we really had had enough after all.

AS FAR AS GUN VIOLENCE was concerned, I could see that nothing was going to change, and Texas politicians certainly weren't going to keep us safe. In the summer of 2021, bowing to a very vocal minority of conservative Second Amendment activists, Governor Greg Abbott signed a bill into law allowing state residents over the age of twenty-one without criminal records to legally carry handguns pretty much anywhere they wanted without a license or training. The law would kick in that September. Prior to that—when I bought my gun for that *GQ* magazine story a few years back—Texas residents needed a license to carry a handgun, but there was nothing to stop an eighteen-year-old from walking into a gun store and buying an AR-15, slinging it over his shoulder, and wandering around downtown Austin showing it off. And a number of times while I lived there, several people did, protesting what they felt was a ludicrous irony in the law by wearing their AR-15s outside the capitol. For these Second Amendment stalwarts, it seemed crazy that the state required them to apply for a license to carry a pistol but not an AR. To them it didn't matter that incidents involving these weapons had, even in recent memory, struck fear into Austinites; back in 2010, Colton Tooley, a nineteen-year-old UT student, had donned a suit and ski mask and ran across campus firing rounds into the air before walking to the sixth floor of the Perry-Castañeda Library and taking his own life. It was the principle of the thing. To those people the Second Amendment was sacrosanct regardless of how many shootings, deaths, or massacres happened.

In 2021, a University of Texas poll showed a solid majority of Texans didn't want permitless carry at all, but that didn't matter. A year later, after the legislature slashed $211 million from the department that oversaw mental health programs, eighteen-year-old Salvador Ramos assassinated nineteen children and two teachers at an elementary school in Uvalde, Texas. And Abbott, without a hint of irony, said the school shooter had a "mental health challenge" and the state needed to "do a better job with mental health." It had nothing to do with access to guns. In fact, even after Uvalde, Abbott made it clear he thought it would be unconstitutional to raise the minimum age for purchasing AR-15s and other assault-style rifles from eighteen to twenty-one years old, despite parents of the victims calling for it.

Vote him out at the ballot box. If that's what new Austinites thought after coming to terms with what had happened a couple of hours away in Uvalde, not to mention the cold, hard fact that since 2012 the state they called home in 2022 had seen more school shootings than any other in America, they were in for some cold, hard truths about Texas politics.

So, in 2019, my family made the decision to leave Texas for good. And this time, I had no reservations. Shannon and I were on the same page as far as why we were leaving. This time we'd sell the house too. I knew moving would be easier for me—I'd already ripped the Band-Aid off when I moved from London to Texas all those years before, leaving friends and family behind. I'd miss our Austin pals, of course, but they'd come and visit us in our new home once we were settled, and we'd come back to visit them. Our reasons for going this time were immutable.

Then it was announced that Olive's school would be closing for good. One Monday morning in November 2019, a bunch of students walked out of Pease Elementary School ahead of a school board meeting that evening at which there was a planned vote to shutter the school. Pease was the first school in Texas built entirely with public money and, until its closure, the oldest continually operating school in the state. It was a diverse school with small class sizes, and the only one in the district that was 100 percent transfer; getting in was a lottery, and all the parents whose kids were successful were invested in it because they'd actually found out about it and applied to send them there. Olive started kindergarten at Pease in August 2016. Parents helped tend the vegetable garden out front; a dad designed and printed "Bobcats" T-shirts to sell at school fundraisers; a group of artist parents painted a huge mural on an outside wall. Everyone got stuck in. The teachers were dedicated and lovely. The kids loved Pease, and the parents did too.

For a while, students in the thousands had been leaving the Austin Independent School District (AISD), their parents choosing to relocate not just to more affordable suburbs but to areas with better schools. Meanwhile, the school district had a $29 million budget deficit in 2018. Its solution? To close twelve schools to save money and slash up to two hundred jobs. Two years earlier, in the spring of 2017, when hundreds of people gathered at the Texas state capitol calling for better funding for Texas public schools, the state ranked twenty-seventh in the nation for public school teacher salaries—they were earning $51,890, around $6,500 below average. One parent compiled data on all the schools the district was looking to close and discovered that the campuses were often overcrowded, underfunded, and in places where families were economically disadvantaged. Three of them had 100 percent enrollment, which seemed to contradict at least one of the reasons that AISD gave for closing them. Eventually, after loud protests from the community, the list of schools identified for closure was reduced to four elementaries. All but Pease was east of I-35. Remember the 1928 city plan? These were diverse schools, and opponents of the closures pointed out that shutting them would disproportionately affect Black and Hispanic students. One was Sims Elementary, which Stephen Galloway, the owner of Galloway Sandwich Shop, attended until seventh grade. Since 2004, enrollment of Black students in the Sims district had declined by 44 percent, and parents worried its closure represented the loss of another of the city's historically Black schools.

Shutting Pease made little sense to anyone whose children actually went there. The associate superintendent Gilbert Hicks even described the school to me as the "jewel in the crown" of AISD. It was the perfect example (in my opinion) of how modernized campuses don't guarantee a better education. Sure, the old stone building could have done with a refurb and the air-conditioning rattled, but Pease felt about as idyllic a community school as you could find, with brilliant teachers, involved parents, and enthusiastic kids. Olyvia Green, who in 1969 was the first Black teacher at Pease, responsible for what she recalled was a diverse third grade class of Black, white, and Hispanic kids, never believed the district would end up shutting the school. "They've been trying to close Pease for years . . ." she said a few years back. "The parents are fighting for the right not to close it . . . Think about the children and the parents." But close it they did.

WHEN LEEANN ATHERTON LEFT HER teaching job at Pease, she left Austin's public school system altogether. Leeann was Olive's music teacher there, a fireball of energy and one of the most inspirational educators I'd ever met. Originally from South Carolina, Leeann, who was a singer-songwriter, moved first to Nashville, but she fell in love with Austin on a road trip, eventually moving to the city permanently in the mid-1980s because it seemed like a more fun place to live. She got a job selling advertising for the *Austin Chronicle* and a part-time gig waitressing in order to fund her main passion in life: music. Eventually Leeann left the *Chronicle* to train to become a teacher. She was a single mother, renting a house in south Austin, and one day, when her son was about a year old, she came home to find a "For Sale" sign in her yard and wondered if it was time for her to try to buy a home for herself. A friend mentioned that a house two doors down was about to go on the market—an older place, built in 1940, on a half-acre plot. She offered to mow the unruly front lawn for the seller and the pair got chatting. Eventually the woman offered to sell the home to Leeann and finance the sale. Leeann's mortgage was $350 a month.

We met one morning in the same house she's lived in ever since. An old upright piano stood in the dark-wood-paneled living room, surrounded by plants, and outside she'd had a makeshift stage built in the corner of her yard where she puts on ad hoc performances with friends. We sat in the kitchen drinking motor-oil coffee. After leaving Pease, she told me, she went to work for a charter school. Today she works with kids with dyslexia. Leeann

wrote a song while she was at Pease that all the students, including Olive, used to sing at school events, gathered under a gigantic
oak in the playground that they'd affectionately named the "Pease
Tree." They could all recite the song by heart. It began: "Underneath the Pease Tree / Where we raise our families," a paean to a
school that was much more than a place where kids learned; the
song spoke of them growing up there, of parents sharing in the values it stood for, and of the school spirit that endured through the
years. Pease had become an identity for these kids; they had
become a little tribe. And that tribe had been disbanded by people
in suits who thought that the jewel in the crown of AISD wasn't
worth preserving. Back in the 1980s, Leeann had sent her son to
Pease. "It was the coolest school," she told me. "Unique, diverse,
cross-cultural. To me, shutting it down is the perfect example for
what you're doing here, why you're writing this book."

LEEANN STILL MAKES MUSIC TODAY, playing mainly to people
who have followed her career since she first came to Austin. In
addition to working a few hours a day with kids with dyslexia,
she has a part-time gig taking tourists on electric bike tours of
the city. She paid her mortgage off a while ago. "That's how I can live
here. I got to Austin when it was still affordable. I couldn't have
made it today on a teacher's salary. Today a handful of musicians
make good money, and then the rest of us make the normal $75
to $100 a night playing a show. And that's a good night. I'm not
sure how they're pulling it off." Leeann says few bars in town will
give musicians what's known as a "guarantee"—a set amount of
cash they'll take home regardless of how many people show up
to watch them. Even though the bar makes money, Leeann says,
either you'll get the cash the bar charges at the door or you have
to survive on tips. "I even knew one songwriter who made jewelry to sell at her gigs, and she made more money selling jewelry

to people who'd come out to listen to music on a weekend. The music was almost like an afterthought."

Times have changed, she thinks; a lot of the new bars cropping up around town aren't focused on music. People just want to go for a drink in their neighborhood instead. "My son's in his thirties. He doesn't even like to go hear live music. He really just wants to go and have a beer. I am passionate about it, though. I wish I could pass this torch on to him."

I wondered how many people moving to Austin actually come for live music anymore. It seems like it's just something that gets reeled off in a list of things that make the city sound cool. That laid-back lifestyle, the hot weather, the lake, and the music scene, all of which have either disappeared, become depleted, or are now unbearable.

CHAPTER 13

THE ELON AND JOE SHOW

I n the spring of 2020, six months after that man carrying an AR-15 walked toward a group of children playing on a splash pad a few blocks from Olive's school, we put our house on the market. It was the middle of a pandemic and possibly not the wisest time to move. But we were ready. Each time a potential buyer came to view the house, Shannon, Olive, Scruff, and I would jump in our camper parked on the driveway and wait. And our realtor friend was right. Within forty-eight hours we had a buyer, and in May we'd be leaving Austin for good.

I can't count the number of times we paused to think: *Are we doing the right thing, making the right move?* Right up until the minute we signed the paperwork, tears streaming down our faces, we questioned everything: our motives for leaving, our motives for moving to the Northeast. I wondered how much of the Austin that I fell in love with almost twenty years earlier still existed and if that was enough to keep us there. I'd hated the London winters, happy to have exchanged them for the heat of Texas, but Austin was hotter and busier and different enough from the place it had been to make me know it was time—and just in time to not let those changes taint my memories of the city.

I also appreciate how relatively easy it was for us to just sell up and go, move across country—or even to the UK if that's where we had decided to go. Yes, it was emotional to leave a place we'd lived in so long and hard to leave friends behind—and navigating the paperwork and real estate agents and lawyers involved in buying and selling property wasn't fun—but I was aware how privileged I was to even own a house that made this possible, to have two passports that meant I could live in either country. To get to Texas, all I'd had to do was apply for a media visa. A few years later I'd married an American, applied for a green card, and eventually got my citizenship. Magali, who probably felt like more of an Austinite than I ever did and who had committed to staying in the city, had to breach the border to get there and then live her life in the shadows. Meanwhile, as Austin got bigger and brasher and more expensive, it had caught the attention of some of the super wealthy: people attracted to this supposedly cool city in the heart of freedom-loving Texas.

JUST AS I WAS SHIPPING out, the podcast host Joe Rogan closed on a $14.4 million, eleven-thousand-square-foot mansion in the city and moved in with his wife and two daughters. The beefy, balding fiftysomething was already insanely famous when he decided to make the move from California to Texas in search of, in his words, "a little bit more freedom," and he'd settled on a Tuscan-style McMansion with Hill Country views, a swimming pool, and a giant wine cellar. Rogan had made his name as an MMA commentator and stand-up comedian before launching a podcast that had become, by the time he got to Austin, the biggest in the US and one of the most popular on the planet. As far as his politics were concerned, Rogan would fit right in. Cable channel Newsmax named him one of the hundred most influential libertarians in America. On his podcast, he'd interviewed

Elon Musk, during which the Tesla founder smoked a blunt, unsheathed a samurai sword, and indulged Rogan in rambling conversations about how governments should regulate artificial intelligence and how to revolutionize transportation. Rogan had also described Austin's Alex Jones as "the most misunderstood guy on the planet," regularly talked enthusiastically about guns, and used the N-word on multiple occasions. He had courted controversial, right-wing figures, embarked on anti-trans rants, and laughed as one of his guests bragged about giving women comedians stage time in exchange for sexual favors.

As the coronavirus spread and the United States went into lockdown, Rogan decided it was "exhausting" watching coverage of the pandemic, because reporters simply used it as a "chance to shit on" President Trump. He cited news coverage of experimental coronavirus treatments—in particular the antimalarial hydroxychloroquine—as an example of what he believed was biased reporting. But his opinions, while controversial, were apparently valuable enough for Spotify to ink a reported $200 million deal with him for the exclusive rights to *The Joe Rogan Experience* podcast. If, as the academic James Rushing Daniel put it, Rogan's "sardonic libertarian-leaning brand of neoliberalism" had ever seemed at odds with Austin's progressive identity in the past, it didn't anymore. Daniel reckoned that in the post-Trump era, Texas was the vanguard of what he called a "hyperreactionary neoliberalism," and Austin, particularly, had embraced it.

In my work as a journalist I'd come across people who thought they knew better than bona fide experts on any given subject, and it was infuriating. It also seemed to me that it correlated with how much money they had: that the richer they were, the greater the chance they were imbued with this notion of intellectual superiority, particularly in subjects of which they had little real knowledge. Austin was now the place to be for these world-changing wannabes. I felt too that the tech industry had an outsized claim to these men—and they were almost always men.

BACK IN 2014, FOR THE *Telegraph* newspaper in London, I interviewed Dave Asprey, founder of the Bulletproof diet. Asprey had worked for Silicon Valley start-ups and made his fortune as a pioneer of cloud computing before he took a trip to Tibet in 2004 that changed his life. He saw how the Sherpas who scaled the mountains surrounding him ate a diet that was high in fat and low in carbs and drank gallons of yak butter tea. "It's the only thing that keeps you going at altitude," he wrote. Adapting the recipe for the American palate, Asprey invented Bulletproof coffee, a mix of full-fat butter, organic coffee, and coconut oil. Soon there were Bulletproof coffee devotees everywhere, desperate to "biohack" their body. Asprey then invented a Bulletproof diet too, which included a lot of butter, red meat, and white rice. It was a diet rich in saturated fats, which the American Heart Association said put you at a higher risk of heart disease. "The only thing I have to say to the American Heart Association," Asprey told me, "is 'Shame on you.'" He claimed to have read "countless thousands" of research papers to come up with the diet, which he says can help "reduce your risks of cancer, heart disease, stroke, diabetes, and Alzheimer's."

Perhaps unsurprisingly, I found that the research papers he posted on his website fell short of backing his diet up; Prof. Paul Garner at the Liverpool School of Tropical Medicine told me the studies were "unreliable . . . highly selective, many over thirty years old, of one or two patients." In fact it was worse than that. A 2004 study found that Tibetans drank high quantities of buttered salt tea, consuming 12.5 percent more calories than the recommended daily allowance, and that these "high amounts of fat and caloric consumption had resulted in increasing obesity among Tibetans, increasing their risk for other health problems." They suffered from digestive disorders, upper respiratory diseases, tuberculosis, arthritis, joint pain, and back pain. Asprey, meanwhile, believed that his Bulletproof diet had "upgraded his brain," ensuring he'll live to be at least 180 years old.

In early 2023, Asprey moved from his thirty-two-acre farm in Canada to Austin, and that summer he announced he'd secured a lease on a property to open Upgrade Labs—what he calls "the world's first Human Upgrade Center"—so Austinites could "witness the evolution of biohacking like never before." Along with Austin's vast, change-everything technology boom came the Dave Aspreys of this world, possessed with an astounding self-belief that if you're a dot-com millionaire, you also happen to have the God-given ability to save the human race.

MASSIVELY SUCCESSFUL TECH ENTREPRENEURS APPEARED, to me at least, to possess a unique brand of arrogance—that by making millions (or billions) in their chosen field, they now had the nous to solve world hunger or help humans live forever. They didn't feel they needed to bankroll people who knew what they were doing, though; they thought they knew what to do themselves. At the time of writing, the most listened-to episodes from Joe Rogan's podcast featured, in fourth place, Alex Jones; in third place, Edward Snowden; in second, a joint appearance between Area 51 conspiracy theorist Bob Lazar and ufologist Jeremy Corbell; and, in first place, Elon Musk.

Musk had already been running SpaceX for almost two decades; the company, which sent astronauts to the International Space Station, now had its sights set on Mars. He had already started the Boring Company to create underground city transit systems and Neuralink to implant devices in the brain to treat disease (and to further "human enhancement"). By the time he chose to move his company Tesla to Austin in 2021, Musk had become equally, if not more, famous for his controversial tweets; he was a divisive figure who seemed to take pleasure in being a contrarian, even if it cost him financially. He seemed like the perfect bedfellow for Rogan. Tesla had announced it was moving its corporate headquarters to Texas in the fall of 2020. For a few years, California had been hemorrhaging residents who had moved to the Lone Star State. One estimate said one in ten new Texans had come from California—the most of any other state. Tesla's Austin factory could produce three times as many vehicles as the one on the West Coast, and ahead of the company's move, Musk said its Texas facility would employ up to twenty thousand people. "Gavin Newsom is U-Haul salesman of the year," Musk joked. While he maintained he's never looked to buy a house in Austin, reports said Musk moved into a luxurious waterfront estate on the banks of the Colorado River beneath Mount Bonnell that belonged to billionaire friend Ken Howery, a cofounder of PayPal.

Musk is an unpredictable controversialist. Like Joe Rogan, during the pandemic, he questioned the science of the virus, tweeting variously that the "pandemic is dumb," that "something extremely bogus is going on" (because he got different results from four COVID tests on the same day), and that it "may be worth considering chloroquine for C19." His take on geopolitics included insisting Taiwan should become a special administrative zone of China, which caused Taiwan's ambassador to the United States to respond that freedom was "not for sale." He tweeted a plan for Ukraine-Russia peace—"Crimea formally part of Russia, as it has been since 1783"—which came under fire for echoing Kremlin talking points. And controversy followed him offline as well. A flight attendant for SpaceX's corporate fleet claimed Musk exposed himself and asked her to perform a sexual favor while she was giving him a massage as part of her duties. Reports said the company bought her silence for $250,000. Musk denied it, calling it a "politically motivated hit piece."

Remember what I said about tech bros and God complexes? An awful lot of people, it transpired, had faith in Musk's ability to do just that too. Antonio Gracias, a close friend of Musk's, said the tech billionaire had the "never-ending drive to change the course of humanity." In 2021, an analysis of Google data revealed that online searches for the question "Could Elon Musk solve world hunger?" had risen by 1,150 percent. It was triggered by a Twitter conversation (what else?) that Musk had engaged in with the director of the World Food Program, who said just 2 percent of Musk's wealth could solve world hunger. Musk responded that if the WFP could describe exactly how those billions would help, he would sell Tesla stock right that moment and do it.

Others took issue with Musk's publicity stunts like launching a $250,000 Tesla Roadster, complete with a plastic human in a spacesuit sitting in the driver's seat, into space via a Falcon Heavy rocket. Musk said he hoped it would float between Earth and Mars for a billion years, but scientists said it would deteriorate over time from the sun's radiation and raised serious questions about space junk. There is also a chance pieces of it that don't burn up upon reentry could come plunging back to Earth one day in populated places. Then, in the summer of 2022, locals in New South Wales, Australia, reported hearing a loud boom before three pieces of space junk plummeted from the heavens and into two separate fields of sheep. Australia's space agency later confirmed the debris belonged to SpaceX.

TODAY, AUSTIN ATTRACTS "BRO SAVIORS" just like Joe Rogan and Elon Musk. After decades spent in Silicon Valley working as an entrepreneur, Tim Ferriss moved to Austin in 2017. A decade

earlier he had published *The 4-Hour Workweek*, a guide to ditch-
ing the nine-to-five and joining the new rich. The book almost
certainly took Ferriss more than four hours a week to write, but
it succeeded in tapping into the frustrations and daydreams of
desk-bound office employees everywhere, made it onto the *New
York Times* bestseller list, and sold more than two million copies. Sound a little too good to be true?

It was.

One of his solutions to never working a nine-to-five again
was to become an expert in the field of your choice—a status he
claimed could be attained in less than a month. Ferriss wrote that
it's fine knowing everything there is to know about medicine, but
without the "MD" at the end of your name, few people will pay you
any attention. He told the story of a friend who took just three
weeks to become a "top relationship expert" featured in national
magazines and who went on to counsel executives at Fortune 500
companies. How did she do it? According to Ferriss, she joined a
handful of trade organizations "with official-sounding names,"
read three bestselling books on the topic, gave a free seminar at
a well-known university, then did the same at two well-known
companies, using the free university gig as a leg up. She wrote
for a few magazines and joined ProfNet, an online service journalists use to source expert quotes on a subject.

But this wasn't a scam. How dare you entertain such thoughts!
Ferriss wasn't recommending *pretending* to be something you're
not (his words). He was merely pointing out that today, proof of
expertise is about media mentions and group affiliations, not
PhDs. One chapter was designed "not for people who want to *run*
businesses but for those who want to *own* businesses and spend
no time on them." Could a business like the Body Shop or Patagonia
change the world? he asked. "Yes, but that isn't our goal here."
Once you've set up your new business, Ferriss recommended out-

sourcing work to "remote assistants" in the developing world for five dollars an hour.

Ferriss's book was immensely popular in Silicon Valley. There are, I'd wager, thousands of copies of *The 4-Hour Workweek* in living rooms all across Austin as well. As one reviewer wrote, he'd created a brand "something like a Tony Robbins geared to the tech set, targeted to young creative people obsessed with efficiency." I wonder how many people gave up their nine-to-five job in order to become a fake expert by joining some trade organizations, reading some books, and giving some seminars, and found it didn't work out? Ferriss, meanwhile, is still doing his thing, but from his new home in Austin.

JOE LONSDALE WAS ANOTHER RECENT transplant to the city. He was the chiseled-jaw, toothpaste-commercial-grin tech entrepreneur and former PayPal executive who had cofounded a controversial data analysis company called Palantir, which provided tech to ICE to aid its efforts to deport undocumented migrants. Lonsdale was also a founding partner of venture capital firm 8VC. In 2012, while serving as a mentor at Stanford, Lonsdale had a relationship with a student, which was prohibited under the university's code of conduct. Stanford temporarily banned Lonsdale from mentoring undergraduates, and separately banned him from campus for a decade after an investigation of the student's allegations of sexual harassment and misconduct. Upon discovery of new evidence in 2015, Stanford reversed the finding of sexual misconduct and harassment and lifted the campus ban. Shortly after moving to Austin with his wife and three young daughters, Lonsdale bought a cowboy hat and boots and obtained a concealed carry gun permit. And he had decided to back a new higher education establishment in Austin, one he very much thought the city needed.

The story goes something like this. In 2021, the former president of a private liberal arts college in Maryland announced he was forming a new institution in Austin. The urgent reason for creating the University of Austin (not to be confused with the University of Texas), Pano Kanelos wrote, was that higher education in America was broken—broken because almost a quarter of his fellow academics across this great nation endorsed the idea of "ousting a colleague for having a wrong opinion about hot-button issues such as immigration or gender differences." More than a third of conservative academics, Kanelos complained, posited that they'd been threatened with disciplinary action for their views. His fix: a new university, based in Austin, where students and faculty could finally say what they really thought, where they could object to affirmative action, vocalize their "un-woke" opinions on race and gender, and stop prioritizing "emotional comfort over the often-uncomfortable pursuit of truth." Kanelos, who described Austin as "like one big maker space now," was saving the American university, and he wasn't doing it alone. He was doing it alongside other academics and those obsessed with "the wind of freedom": people like Niall Ferguson, the controversial British historian known for his support of British imperialism; Kathleen Stock, a philosophy professor who quit the University of Sussex in the UK after being accused of transphobia; and Joe Lonsdale, who believed he too was the victim of the very kind of cancel culture this super new university was built to oppose.

Austin University was also the brainchild of Bari Weiss, a journalist who had worked as an op-ed editor at both the *Wall Street Journal* and *New York Times*. Weiss had famously resigned from the *Times* in a letter published on her website claiming the newspaper regularly caved to the Twitter mob. "Twitter is not on the masthead of *The New York Times*. But Twitter has become its ultimate editor," she wrote. The fact that Weiss was behind Austin University shouldn't have shocked anyone. In 2018, she'd written an opinion piece for the *Times* titled "Meet the Renegades of the Intellectual Dark Web" in which she discussed "iconoclastic thinkers, academic renegades and media personalities" who felt "largely locked out of legacy [media] outlets." These included Dave Rubin, whose talk show *The Rubin Report* he called "a hub for misunderstood or canceled people ... to express themselves honestly." (Rubin once described progressivism as a "mental disorder.") The University of Austin was built, Weiss said, "for witches who refuse to burn." Referring to its new home in the Texas capital, the university's website read: "If it's good enough for Elon Musk and Joe Rogan, it's good enough for us."

Of course, many were skeptical. Katelyn Burns, the first ever openly trans Capitol Hill reporter, writing for MSNBC, said the University of Austin "appears to be the latest, and largest, in a long line of cancel culture–related grifts." She noted that none of the academics were expected to produce research, none of the programs provided credits accepted at actual colleges, and instead it appeared "to be a clearinghouse for online videos or classes, where people ... can say whatever [they want] about trans people or ... lecture about racial IQ without official consequences."

Initially, the university was to be a space for students to take informal online courses; eventually it would have a physical campus in Austin that could accommodate up to four thousand people. But two weeks after the announcement of the launch of this anti–cancel culture school of learning, two of its notable advisory board members—University of Chicago chancellor Robert Zimmer and Harvard professor Steven Pinker—unceremoniously announced they were leaving. "As is often the case with fast-moving start-ups, there were some missteps," a statement by the university read. Today, it's still seeking authorization from the Texas Higher Education Coordinating Board to offer degrees and in the process of pursuing official accreditation.

CHAPTER 14

FREEDOM AND
THE FUTURE

Living in Austin felt enough like a bubble that you could *almost* believe that the things happening there hadn't happened before, like the city hadn't changed and become steadily less accessible long before you arrived. That's how I felt, anyway, and Dowell Myers's study was sort of remarkable for showing that everything happening today in Austin was . . . familiar. It showed the impact the 1970s and early '80s tech boom, with its sudden and furious injection of capital into the economy, caused—not just on the music scene but on the water we used in Austin for drinking and recreation. But it also showed that because of the economic crash in the mid-'80s, a lot of the dire predictions luckily didn't materialize. The slump effectively paused the detrimental effect all that growth was having on the city. The music scene recovered. The environment got a reprieve.

This time around, though, I wondered, *Is it too late?* Even if we go into a deep recession, even if Austin experiences the inevitable economic peaks and troughs, has the horse already bolted? I thought of other cities like Detroit and San Francisco, where rapid growth had changed the city indelibly. How do you go back when a place is still catching up to the expectations attached to it? Suffering from them?

I decided to talk to Myers about his original study, to look at the different assets that Austin boasted back then and revisit them today. The state capitol, for example, was a driver of the economy back in the '80s and still is today, through tourism, government agencies and departments, lobbyists and lawyers. But it also houses a legislature that has shifted so far to the right it's in danger of frightening away the very people and companies it was desperate to attract. I wondered, all these decades on, whether Myers saw the "capitol" as an albatross rather than an asset.

He said in the decades since the era of LBJ and Governor Ann Richards, Texas had succeeded in creating an "anti-California culture," which has alienated highly educated people working in innovative technology that Austin had fought so hard to encourage to the city. And because house prices are escalating, he said, Austin was no longer this incredibly affordable alternative to California either. What's more, anyone who lived through—or watched from afar—the effect the big freeze had on the state's infrastructure would have second-guessed their decision or any contemplation to move there. Texas no longer seemed resilient or reliable. "Austin's on shaky ground," Myers told me.

FOR NEWCOMERS TO THE CITY, their Republican governor's reaction to the COVID-19 pandemic may have been one of the first things to cause alarm bells. He left it up to schools to decide whether pupils should stay home. He closed restaurants, gyms, and movie theaters, then he reopened them and closed them again. Hospitals became overwhelmed. Then, on March 2, 2021, a year after the pandemic hit, Abbott lifted all state-imposed occupancy limits and mask mandates. At the time the state's death toll stood at 44,811, with 5,508 people hospitalized. Abbott argued Texans knew how to protect themselves by that point. It was a similar policy toward power providers that would get so much criticism after the polar vortex hit Texas in February 2021. Still under fire for relaxing restrictions while the pandemic was raging, Abbott now blamed wind and solar power and the Green New Deal (which was never signed into law) for problems that were in fact the fault of deregulation: the belief that government shouldn't involve itself too much in the response to the largest pandemic since AIDS, and it shouldn't regulate power companies either. Texans know what to do to protect themselves. Power companies know what to do to keep the electricity flowing. The mantra from those pulling the political strings was this: Government shouldn't interfere. Freedom is paramount. You're on your own. Except, of course, when it comes to women and what they wanted to do with their bodies.

In 2017, a bill was passed banning the most common procedure used for second-trimester abortions, and it required clinics and hospitals to cremate or bury fetal remains. That law, eventually blocked by a district judge, also extended to ectopic pregnancies and miscarriages. Almost a year before the Supreme Court overturned *Roe v. Wade,* Texas had enacted one of the most extreme abortion restrictions in the country when Abbott signed into law a measure banning the procedure whenever a "fetal heartbeat" was detected, which could be as early as six weeks, before most women even know they're pregnant. The law also applied to women who had become pregnant through rape or incest, and it allowed for private citizens to sue abortion providers and doctors, essentially offering a $10,000 reward for informants. The law effectively shut down most abortion clinics in the state.

Bills like that one spurred on other, deeply conservative bills. In 2021, the legislature passed a bill requiring student athletes to play on sports teams that corresponded to the gender on their birth certificate in order, it said, to "protect girls' safety." The following year Abbott ordered the Texas Department of Family and Protective Services to investigate parents of transgender children, claiming certain medical procedures and other treatment amounted to child abuse. He also signed sweeping voting legislation that, according to legal challenges, restricted voting access for mainly Black and brown people as well as disabled voters, banning, for example, early-hours and drive-through voting, popular with voters of color in Harris County, which is known for its diverse electorate. Democrats said it amounted to voter suppression in a state whose voting system was already seen as one of the most restrictive in the nation. Abbott insisted it would ensure election integrity.

Republicans outlawed the teaching of critical race theory—a decades-old academic concept taught in law school that looks at how racism extends to political, legal, and social structures like the criminal justice system, housing, and health care—in the state's K–12 public school classrooms. And they introduced tax and other financial penalties designed to punish any Texas city that "defunded the police."

And yet, in November 2022, Abbott and his fellow Texas Republicans maintained a grip on state government that they'd had for almost thirty years and began doubling down on their assault on LGBTQ+ folk. They introduced ten bills designed to criminalize gender-affirming care for transgender young people, ban transgender kids from competing in sports events, curb discussion of sexual orientation and gender identity in schools, and criminalize drag shows.

The revered writer Molly Ivins, who once edited the *Texas Observer*, described the Texas legislature as "the finest free entertainment in Texas. Better than the zoo. Better than the circus," and said Texas Republicans came "in two flavors: conservative and extraordinary." But if right-wing Texas politicians were once funny, the laws they were enacting today weren't. I think the big question now is this: Will those Austinites who moved to the state less than a decade ago choose to leave once the realization sets in that Austin is actually firmly situated in Texas, and that changing the state's political leaders may take decades? Will companies refuse to move to Austin when they understand that zero state income tax means financially supporting—in other ways—right-wing policies they profoundly disagree with? And will companies already there decide they've had enough?

IN 2021, THE CEOs OF twenty-eight Austin companies signed an open letter to Texas lawmakers with the heading: "Don't Mess with Texas' Innovation. It's not fair, it's not democracy, and it's not good for business." The letter, from people like Tyson Tuttle of Silicon Labs, Michael Patton from the package delivery company Fetch, and Hugh Forrest, chief programming officer of SXSW, said that while Texas was known for being one of America's most business-friendly states, its government was busy finding legal loopholes in order to "skirt around national laws and suppress voters they don't agree with." It noted that computer giant Oracle as well as Tesla, SpaceX, Neuralink, and the Boring Company had all moved to Texas; that Apple's second headquarters was expanding in Austin; and that new investors and venture capitalists now called the state home: "Texas has undisputedly won in tech during the very challenging pandemic." But they said while Abbott, and Rick Perry before him, had successfully recruited companies to the state, in the past few months they'd witnessed disturbing new laws passed and executive orders issued that threatened to "kill the Golden Goose of growth that we've been enjoying for so long."

The CEOs pointed specifically to laws they said made it harder to vote, especially for lower-income people and people of color; laws that allowed almost anyone to openly carry firearms without training or a permit; and laws that targeted transgender children. And they noted that software giant Salesforce, with a market capitalization of more than $255 billion, had already told its one-thousand-strong Texas workforce it would pay relocation expenses for any employees "wanting to flee our state." Following Texas's strict abortion law coming into effect, Apple CEO Tim Cook told his employees that their health insurance would help cover costs for travel outside the state if they needed to seek an abortion. "We will see more announcements like this if we don't change course," the letter said.

IN VIEW OF LEGISLATION LIKE that, I wondered whether Austin's laid-back lifestyle was enough of a draw anymore. In his original study, Dowell Myers described the "summer heat" and "slower pace of activity" as key attributes encouraging companies to move there. Maybe back then summer heat didn't sound oppressive. I asked whether, if he was conducting his study today, it would still be a positive attribute. "I think it has been a liability really," he said. Back in the 1980s, the Austin lifestyle centered around community swimming pools where people could cool down at the end of the day. Air-conditioning wasn't universal. Today, he said, air-conditioning has separated people from community. But he told me it was important to maintain some perspective: Austin isn't as hot as Phoenix or Palm Springs, after all. I'm not sure that kind of perspective would sway me today. Yes, Phoenix endured the hottest summer ever measured in 2023—fifty-four days over 110 degrees Fahrenheit—but Austin had its second hottest. The first was the year Olive was born.

The biggest difference in the Austin lifestyle is this: what Austin has gained in the years since Myers's study, like fantastic, world-class restaurants and alternatives to watching live bands, such as movie theaters, bowling alleys, and skating rinks, no longer set it apart as a big city. If twenty years ago Austin's schtick was its live music scene, its Tex-Mex and barbecue restaurants, its low-rise, recognizable skyline, and laid-back river and lakeside living, those special qualities have now been replaced by things that any city its size could boast. So if Austin is no different from any other city of its size, then prospective employees, instead of wondering what sets this city apart, might only wonder how much they'll get paid if they move there.

In the past, wages were always lower in places like California because everybody wanted to move to California. In the same way, you didn't have to pay top dollar to persuade someone to come to Austin because everyone wanted to come to Austin. But I'd bet people moving to Austin today still reel off the things it was famous for in the past; that in conversations with friends and family they conjure a romantic image of the city they've chosen as their new home: the great music scene, the barbecue, the sparkling lakes— even if the reality is that the music scene is a shell of its former self, they'll be lucky to get a table at the restaurant they want to go to, and the lake is partially dried up. Because, as Myers pointed out, "Austin in the absence of Barton Springs is just tumbleweeds. Those little symbolic things are important. And the absence of them is going to change the migration streams."

Austin's skyline has changed. There's no going back. Communities of color have been driven from the east side. The impacts of climate change are all but unstoppable. So what is Austin's future? If the laid-back atmosphere and its music scene were a huge part of its appeal and that's been flipped on its head, can you claw back what you've lost—that magic that people who have never even been to Austin heard it possessed? "You can't reverse it," Myers told me, "but you can prolong its decline." And if you manage to do that, any further negative changes will be less perceptible, and it'll allow people living there to adjust.

If there's a set of keys to Austin's future, it, unfortunately, is in the hands of the same people who threw fuel on the fire that stoked its unprecedented growth in the first place: those who decided to encourage urban regeneration, who put together those packages of tax breaks and zoning measures and incentives that drew tech companies to the city, who shifted Austin's purpose from providing for the poor and middle classes to creating wealth for the rich. But politicians are often interested in making decisions only for the short term—just long enough to cover their time in office. Luckily there's another set of keys to the city's future. Austin needs a vision that involves more than politicians; it needs the people who call it home to think about what it's going to be like in ten and in twenty years' time. And those people need to not only preserve the good things the city already has but identify what it needs—what's missing—and how to get that too.

But what if things have already progressed too much to get those things back?

BY MARCH 2022, DESPITE TEXAS relaxing COVID-19 restrictions much earlier than other parts of the country, remote work was still a common occurrence. This meant office occupancy was worryingly low, and by that November, *Austin Business Journal* wondered "Has Austin Built Too Many Office Towers?" Los Angeles developer Kilroy Realty Corporation announced it had stopped construction on its Stadium Tower next to the city's soccer stadium in north Austin, saying it wanted to wait until the economy improved or it managed to pre-lease a substantial portion of the building. Then Meta, Facebook's parent company, backed out of a plan to occupy almost six hundred thousand square feet of one of Austin's tallest skyscrapers at Sixth and Guadalupe (the building that had cast a shadow, literally and metaphorically, over one of the city's oldest buildings), revealing it would sublease that office space instead. Elsewhere, companies were making job cuts. By November 2022, Austin had more than 64 million square feet of office space available to rent, but around 6 million square feet was still being built. The amount of vacant office space was predicted to rise as working from home became the norm and businesses continued to hire remote staff.

Dr. Harold Hunt, a research economist at Texas A&M University, told me most employers want their people back in the office, but there's resistance from employees. When Elon Musk said his staff must work from the office, a large number quit on him. Hunt pointed to a recent study that said 90 percent of office employees wanted to work remotely or on a hybrid model, but his long-term prediction is that new offices will just poach the commercial occupants from older office blocks built in the '70s and '80s, which may be iconic or beautiful but are functionally obsolete. What then do we do with those '70s and '80s office buildings that are now empty? In a lot of cases it'll be cost prohibitive to convert them into accommodation. And if you can't turn them into condos, what will you do with them? Besides, this is Texas, and why would you pay a fortune to live in a 1,000-square-foot apartment downtown when you could live in a 2,500-square-foot house with a yard outside of Austin for the same price?

PERHAPS PART OF THE ANSWER to the question of how Austin can conjure up some of the alchemy it has lost as it's grown is to go back to the beginning, to look at who the first victims of gentrification are in any city. If we begin by acknowledging what happened to those families, is it then possible to undo some of that damage? Perhaps Austin's destiny as an inequitable city isn't already written in the glass-and-concrete skyscrapers and condos. Maybe it's not just written in the traffic and the lack of public transport, the latter of which continues to push lower-earning people from the city limits.

In the summer of 2021, the city council voted to move ahead
with a developer on a project to build hundreds of affordable homes
as part of a mixed-use development in north Austin's St. John
neighborhood, a historically African American community that
was established by emancipated slaves in the late 1800s. Back in
2008, the city wanted to build a police substation and courthouse
on a nineteen-acre lot there, but Greg Casar, then a neighborhood
campaigner before becoming a city councilman and now US representative, described it as "an investment in punishment, and not
an investment in housing, parks, jobs and childcare." Public pressure spearheaded by Casar ended that idea, and the subsequent
design for the new development included seventy low-income
units. It was part of Austin's new Right to Stay and Right to Return
policy, which offered low-income people, and particularly Black
families with historic ties to the neighborhood who had been or
were at risk of being displaced, the chance to move back to the city
by offering them affordable housing. Proponents of Right to Stay
and Right to Return want to see the model rolled out across Austin,
to see public land owned by the city expanded and protected and
not sold off cheaply to developers concerned solely with substantial profit margins.

Today there is a majority of city councillors who are "pro-
density." This is essentially an opposition to sprawl, an opposition
to single-family homes stretching from the outskirts of town to
the suburbs and beyond—a sea of quarter-acre lots that means
more cars on the road, more grass to be mowed, more electricity
burned. But building downtown condos isn't the best solution to
sprawl. They cost far more per square foot to build than single-
family homes because of the construction techniques used. In
2022, Austin's city councillors wrote that they believed there was
now consensus to increase housing capacity, particularly affordable housing, and invest in transit. But what does this mean if it
doesn't mean condos? It means more town houses or duplexes

instead of single-family homes; it means mixed-income housing and creating walkable and bikeable neighborhoods.

At the tail end of 2022, Austinites voted in favor of a $350 million affordable housing bond—the largest the city had ever seen. The vote in favor was around 70 to 30 percent to fund through taxes the planning, design, construction, and improving of affordable housing facilities, in addition to buying up land to build more. This of course means an increase in property taxes, which presumably is why 30 percent voted against it, but Mayor Steve Adler said it was crucial, as the city was "hemorrhaging people [and] losing a lot of the diversity." The main group lobbying against it was Save Austin Now, which had come to prominence the previous year by campaigning to reinstate the homeless camping ban. Its cofounder, GOP consultant Matt Mackowiak, complained it would saddle taxpayers with $300 million of debt.

Then there's the transportation question. Currently the only rail line for Austinites to use is one that goes from the Austin Convention Center east across I-35, before heading north toward Highway 45 and northwest to Leander, where it ends. It doesn't go to the university. It doesn't go to the airport. It doesn't serve south Austin. Or east Austin. Or west. In 2020, though, Austin voters approved a $7 billion project that, over the next twelve years, promised to expand bus and rail links across the city by growing the existing red line, launching a second commuter train, two light rail lines, and a tunnel. Project Connect, as it was known, would see the rail line service the airport, finally, and expand the existing north-south service. There was also a not-inconsequential $300 million set aside to help those living in what's been termed the "active displacement risk area"—people living near where the light rail line will be built. It's unclear, exactly, how the fund will help them. Their property taxes will inevitably go up, as will the value of their homes, but state law forbids the money to help pay property taxes. The answer from the city is a vague "programs to help preserve home ownership opportunities," which will apparently come in the form of nonprofits.

Perhaps predictably, Project Connect has derailed since it was announced. Costs kept escalating, and by the spring of 2022, estimated figures for the light rail portion alone had ballooned from $5.8 billion to $10.3 billion owing to the significant increase in the cost of land. But planners are not asking taxpayers for more money. Instead, the project has just been downsized and delayed. By March 2023, there were five options on the table, each one showing plans for half the length of the original rail line. There was no more downtown subway, and only one of those new proposals saw a rail link serving the airport. Austin's growth and crazy real estate market meant that a plan to fix one of the very problems caused by that growth was being stymied by that growth, which had caused costs to escalate.

MANY PEOPLE MOVING TO AUSTIN today probably experience that same awe-inducing feeling of excitement. *This is it,* they think. *This is the place for me.* It's not like what Luke and I felt on our journey was particularly unique, and it's not necessarily that Austin has lost its magic altogether. But I do believe it's lost its identity.

A city can change and develop, but the consequences of rapid growth are dire. To grow so fast makes a city unaffordable, and the real thing you lose in a city growing too fast is its people. The people inform the identity of a city. You grow too fast, and homogenization is bound to happen; cities will turn into replicas of one another. And stories are starting to emerge of tech workers, lured to Austin by favorable taxes and a lower cost of living, now reconsidering that move. Some feel that the city was oversold to them and that they're now confronting extreme weather, clogged roads, overcrowding, and a tech scene that failed to live up to the hype.

Maybe that tech boom has already killed the goose that laid the golden egg, that created that "magic" in Austin. But just maybe technology also offers solutions for Austin's future. What if technology could make the city more livable, more equitable? Remember my friend Kevin Ashton, who coined the term "Internet of Things" to describe the concept that physical devices, vehicles, buildings, and more could be connected to the internet in order to run more efficiently? Kevin came up with the term not as a way to describe how your fridge connected to an app so you could tell if your salad was a bit too cold. IoT was not about controlling your household appliances. Kevin had a far bigger vision of entire cities—"Smart cities"—connected to the internet so we could monitor in real time what was happening with infrastructure, with the amount of water released from a dam, with the quality of that water going into people's houses. Smart cities would reduce consumption and costs and be better for the environment. Kevin once told me the easiest analogy for IoT is our nervous system: We have a number of sensors so that we can detect temperature, whether we feel sick, whether we're standing up or sitting down. We get multiple sources of information about the same thing flowing to one place where we can correlate and compare, and that gives us a comprehensive picture of the world around us. This, he thinks, is what the cities of the future will be able to do. So what could that mean for Austin? Flood mitigation, cheaper electricity bills, no traffic on the roads, better access to health care, improved public safety, and more sustainable practices for the city of Austin.

My friend Fred Schmidt, an entrepreneur who's called Austin home for decades, believes the "buzz, the excitement, the fun" of any city is set by its artists, writers, and musicians and cafés and galleries and all those who frequent them. "And then the gentrification treadmill begins," he says, "and the developers move in and all that stuff disappears." But Fred thinks that it creates the impetus for new and interesting places to grow, from small communities to towns nearby and maybe farther afield. "There are tons of really wonderful next-tier cities—new Austins waiting to be discovered—with a great quality of life and a new buzz. And so my prediction is just follow the musicians, follow where they're going, 'cause they're bringing the party with them," Fred said. "They are the curators and the holders of the cultural content of a place, and wherever the artists and the musicians go, that's where everybody else will follow." It's an optimistic prediction, but the truth is if we don't understand how to stop that "gentrification treadmill," then the same thing that's happened to Austin will happen to these other places too.

A LIFETIME AGO, IN 1981, the *Washington Post* asked, "Is Austin growing too fast?" Critics were calling the rapid development of its watersheds a disaster waiting to happen, predicting its city services would struggle. "The old days are gone," it concluded, "and the merchants of growth ride strong." I'm acutely aware that I've contributed to Austin's growth. After that road trip in 1999, I told anyone who would listen about this city that I'd discovered and how it was unlike any other place I'd been. I wrote a travel piece (dripping with hyperbole) for the *Evening Standard*. "The live music capital of the world claim may seem a little lofty," I said, but "Austin hosts more rock bands per square foot than anywhere else in the universe." And that it was "like an oasis, nestled in a sea of hills and green trees." In 2014, I was ecstatic that British Airways had launched the first ever transatlantic flight from Austin to London's Heathrow Airport.

How did I feel now that I was abandoning this city whose growth I had been involved in? Conflicted, honestly. I'll always love Austin, and I want to see it succeed. The way I feel is not unlike that of the friends and loved ones who've stayed in Austin, who still believe in its future. I owe Austin for some of the most significant parts of my life. It's where I met the love of my life, where our daughter was born, where we forged lifelong friendships with some of the most wonderful people on the planet, and where I had the privilege of getting to know so many brilliant and talented journalists determined to make sense of this crazy, newsworthy state and its capital.

As much as I love Austin—and, at times, miss it—I don't see us going back there. For me at least, that magic has worn thin. And I don't see it coming back. If its political leaders had the foresight to look into its past, at what happened before, they would know what they needed to do—or not do—to halt the things that change a city in all the wrong ways. But those who oversee the city's care and development have failed to turn Austin into an equitable, livable city. It's failed to be the place that so many people, for so long, gravitated toward, many of whom have now been forced out.

At the time of writing, rents had started to go down. We don't know what will happen in the coming years, but if Austin became an affordable place to live again it would be a start. I genuinely believe that people create the cultural identity of a city. I loved what I was buying into in 1999, and the reporting I've done for this book often reminded me of how brilliant and wonderful the people of Austin are. Some things I loved about the city are still there, but the question becomes: For how much longer? How long can people who love a city survive in it when it's growing too quickly for everyone besides those at the top? I've joined the ranks of people saying that Austin's not the way it used to be. I often think back to that sweltering summer of Luke's and my road trip, how it felt when we were getting lost in Austin. Now, I have come to believe it's Austin that's gotten lost.

ACKNOWLEDGMENTS

Huge thanks to my agent Howard Yoon, without whom this book wouldn't have happened; my brilliant editor Anna Montague, her assistant Chelsea Herrera, and all the crew at Dey St.; my meticulous fact checker Ethan Bien; Kyle Triplett at New York Public Library; Jennifer Hecker and the rest of the staff at the Austin History Center; Luke Perring, who discovered Austin with me many moons ago; and Shannon and Olive, who made it home.

Thanks also to:

Talib Abdullahi, Art Acevedo, Kevin Ashton, Leeann Atherton, Awais Azhar, Crail Bench, Eric Benson, Marcia Ball, Peter Beck, Ben Carrington, the Case and Baker family, Cherry Chainsaw, Stevie Chick, Nancy Coplin, Amy Concilio, Michael Corcoran, Neil and Leslie Curran, Rob D'Amico, Matt Daddona, John T. Davis, Troy Dillinger, Dwight Dugan, Ted Eubanks, Rachel Feit, Gordon Fowler, Stephen Galloway, Kendra Garrett, Richard Garriott, Alan Graham, Garett and Breanna Gray, Steve Gullick, Cody Haltom, John Hardin, Harold Hunt, Roy Johnson, Jeff Klein, Joey Lazeren, Sharlene Leurig, Nelson Linder, Magali, Luke and Denise Miller, Mike Miller, Mike Mordecai, Blaine Morgan, Dowell Myers, Ritch Napierkowski, Paul Oveisi, Eli and Kenna Pancamo, Tracy LaQuey Parker, Charles Peveto, Forrest Preece,

Matt Rainwaters, Ian and Jane Randolph, Abby Rapoport, Jessica Rush, Jeff Rotkoff, Fred Schmidt, Brent Schumacher, Gardner Selby and the Politimigas gang, Brigid Shea, Tim Shea, Will Sheff, Chris Simpson, Angela Stroud, Eric Tang, Mike Tolleson, Candace Volz, David Waltzer, Forrest Wilder, and Ben Wright.

BIBLIOGRAPHY

Akers, Monte. *Flames After Midnight: Murder, Vengeance, and the Desolation of a Texas Community*. Austin: University of Texas Press, 2011.

Auyero, Javier, ed. *Invisible in Austin: Life and Labor in an American City*. Austin: University of Texas Press, 2015.

Bakeless, John. *America as Seen by Its First Explorers: The Eyes of Discovery*, rev. ed. Dover Publications, 2011.

Baker, Jean. *Schizophrenia: Evolving from My Son's Suicide to the Classroom: A Mother Relates Her Story of Surviving Her Son's Mental Illness and Fulfilling Her Quest to Teach Special Needs Children*. CreateSpace, 2013.

Barnes, Michael. *Indelible Austin: Selected Histories*. Austin: Waterloo Press, 2015.

Boller Jr., Paul F. *Presidential Campaigns: From George Washington to George W. Bush*. New York: Oxford University Press, 2004.

Brogan, Hugh. *The Pelican History of the United States of America*. Harmondsworth: Penguin Books, 1986.

Brown, Dee. *The American West*. New York: Touchstone, 1995.

Cantrell, Gregg. *Stephen F. Austin: Empresario of Texas*. New Haven: Yale University Press, 2001.

Carson, Rachel L., *Silent Spring*. Boston: Houghton Mifflin, 1962.

Crisp, Margie. *River of Contrasts: The Texas Colorado*. College Station: Texas A&M University Press, 2012.

Dobie, J. Frank. *Tales of Old-Time Texas*. Austin: University of Texas Press, 1984.

Dooley-Awbrey, Betty, and Stuart Awbrey. *Why Stop? A Guide to Texas Roadside Historical Markers*. Lanham, MD: Taylor Trade Publishing, 2013.

Eisen, Jonathan, and Harold Straughn. *Unknown Texas*. New York: Collier Books, 1988.

Endres, Clifford. *Austin City Limits*. Austin: University of Texas Press, 1987.

Fehrenbach, T. R. *Lone Star: A History of Texas and the Texans*. New York: Black Dog & Leventhal Publishers, 2007.

Frank, Robert. *The High-Beta Rich: How the Manic Wealthy Will Take Us to the Next Boom, Bubble, and Bust*. New York: Crown Business, 2011.

Graves, John. *Goodbye to a River: A Narrative*. New York: Vintage Departures, 2002.

Haley, James L. *Stephen F. Austin and the Founding of Texas*. New York: Rosen Publishing Group, Inc., 2003.

Hollandsworth, Skip. *The Midnight Assassin: The Hunt for America's First Serial Killer*. New York: Picador, 2017.

Ivins, Molly. *Molly Ivins Can't Say That, Can She?* New York: Vintage, 1992.

Kerr, Jeffrey Stuart. *Austin, Texas, Then and Now: A Photography Scrapbook*. Austin: Promised Land Books, 2004.

Kerr, Jeffrey Stuart. *Seat of Empire: The Embattled Birth of Austin, Texas*. Lubbock: Texas Tech University Press, 2013.

Kingston, Mike. *A Concise History of Texas*. Dallas: Dallas Morning News, 1988.

Lusted, Marcia Amidon, ed. *Gentrification and the Housing Crisis*. New York: Greenhaven Publishing, 2018.

Maslin, Mark. *Climate Change: A Very Short Introduction*. Oxford: Oxford University Press, 2021.

Mehta, Suketu. *Maximum City: Bombay Lost and Found*. New York: Alfred A. Knopf, 2005.

Miller, Todd. *Border Patrol Nation: Dispatches from the Front Lines of Homeland Security*. San Francisco: City Lights Books, 2014.

Minutaglio, Bill, and W. Michael Smith. *Molly Ivins: A Rebel Life*. New York: PublicAffairs, 2009.

Moore, Stephen L. *Taming Texas: Captain William T. Sadler's Lone Star Service*. Austin: State House Press, 2000.

Moskowitz, P. E., *How to Kill a City: Gentrification, Inequality, and the Fight for the Neighborhood*. New York: Bold Type Books, 2017.

Nye, David E. *When the Lights Went Out: A History of Blackouts in America*. Cambridge, MA: MIT Press, 2013.

Patoski, Joe Nick. *Austin to ATX: The Hippies, Pickers, Slackers, and Geeks Who Transformed the Capital of Texas*. College Station: Texas A&M University Press, 2019.

Pearce, Fred. *When the Rivers Run Dry: Water—The Defining Crisis of the Twenty-First Century*. Boston: Beacon Press, 2018.

Reisner, Marc, *Cadillac Desert: The American West and Its Disappearing Water*. New York: Penguin Books, 1993.

Schuerman, Matthew L. *Newcomers: Gentrification and Its Discontents*. Chicago: University of Chicago Press, 2019.

Stroud, Angela. *Good Guys with Guns: The Appeal and Consequences of Concealed Carry*. Chapel Hill: University of North Carolina Press, 2016.

Tretter, Eliot M. *Shadows of a Sunbelt City: The Environment, Racism, and the Knowledge Economy in Austin*. Athens, GA: University of Georgia Press, 2016.

Utley, Robert M. *The Indian Frontier, 1846–1890*. Albuquerque: University of New Mexico Press, 2003.

Walker, Richard A. *Pictures of a Gone City: Tech and the Dark Side of Prosperity in the San Francisco Bay Area*. Oakland: PM Press, 2018.

Wright, Lawrence. *God Save Texas: A Journey into the Soul of the Lone Star State*. New York: Knopf Doubleday Publishing Group, 2018.

ABOUT THE AUTHOR

Alex Hannaford is an award-winning journalist who has written about crime, the death penalty, religion, refugees, and the Mexico border for publications including British *GQ*, *The Guardian & Observer*, *The Sunday Times*, *The Sunday Telegraph*, *The Atlantic*, and *The Texas Observer*. He cowrote and hosted the investigative podcast series *Dead Man Talking*, and wrote and directed *The Last 40 Miles*, an award-winning animated short film about the death penalty. Alex is a Fellow of the Dart Center for Journalism & Trauma at Columbia University. He lives in New York.